Second Chances and Second Cups

Donna Schlachter

Second Chances and Second Cups

Copyright © 2015 Donna Schlachter

All rights reserved.

ISBN:1943688044

ISBN-13: 978-1-943688-04-3

Acknowledgments

So many of these stories were generated through stories told in my family. And through stories not told. In particular, Purple Hyacinths contains some truths about my mother's birth. The Sun Through The Clouds holds truths my father's mother told me. Ten Fingers and Ten Toes is part of a story my mother's mother told me. There are many other stories that have found their way into this book through a character, a phrase, a description of a coffee setting.

But that's what makes story. Nothing specific, but a general collection of facts, of information, of wisdom.

I hope you enjoy these sweet stories that speak about good friends, family, and second chances.

Because all the glory goes to the God of Second Chances, the One True God.

Without Him, there would be no story worth telling.

Please follow me on Facebook and Twitter, and feel free to contact me through my website: www.LiveByTheWord.com

You can also follow my historical blog at www.HiStoryThruTheAges.wordpress.com

I'd appreciate if you'd post an honest review at Amazon, NOOK, Smashwords, and Goodreads.

Sincerely,

Donna Schlachter

Purple Hyacinths

Grace turned at the sound of footsteps on the stairway leading from the second floor. Her granddaughter Tory entered the room, smiling. She reached toward the young woman, and they stood holding hands for some moments, relaxing in the closeness of their relationship. Always the best of friends, sharing secrets, giggling like school girls, they supported each other through many difficult times and shared many warm memories.

And to think that she had nearly given all of this up.

"Nana Grace, let's go out in the back yard, and watch the florist set up." Tory suggested. "I was very careful not to pick any colors that would clash with the flowers in your garden."

Nana Grace smiled, and, linking her wrinkled old

arm in her granddaughter's smooth young one, they walked together out to the back yard. It was a beautiful day, all the more so because this was her only granddaughter's wedding day.

Together they sat at a small glass-topped table under a canvas covering and sipped coffee from delicate cups that Grace had inherited from her own mother. The tiny hand-painted roses against the still-brilliant white china offset the blue sky and green grass to perfection.

Grace raised her cup to her granddaughter. "I've sat here many mornings and drank my morning coffee, listening to the birds." She tipped her head to one side. "There is a nest of cardinals in that tree over there." She pointed. "And in the hedge at the end of the garden, you might see some rabbits."

Tory set her cup down. "I don't know why, but coffee always tastes better when I drink it outdoors." She traced the pattern on the saucer with a forefinger. "Or maybe it's the company."

Grace smiled. "Everything seems sweeter when you're here." She pointed to the notepad on the table at Tory's elbow. "So, tell me about your plans for today."

Her granddaughter filled her in on everything, even though Grace, who always liked to be at the center of activity, knew the schedule by heart. The caterer was setting up in the kitchen overlooking the massive expanse of lawn at the rear of the house, where the wedding and reception were due to take place in just under two hours.

The rest of the bridal party was upstairs, putting the final touches to their outfits. The florist was installing the arrangements in the house and in the gazebo, where the actual ceremony was to be conducted. The small round structure was perfect for the affair, as it was open on all sides, raised above the lawn, and just the right size to hold the wedding party. Guests would be seated on folding chairs arranged around the gazebo.

As she listened to Tory, the morning breeze carried a familiar fragrance, vaguely reminding her of another time and another place. She was still trying to place the scent when Tory spoke.

"See, Nana Grace, your garden is filled with those lovely yellow roses, white daisies, and pale lavender peonies. So, I chose purple hyacinths and baby's breath for my flowers. Mom said that you used to have purple hyacinths in your garden. I thought they would make a wonderful accent. What do you think?"

Purple hyacinths? She hadn't seen or smelled purple hyacinths in over twenty years…

It was a time when people counted backwards on their fingers from the baby's birth date to the wedding date. In this case, there was no doubt. Married in January, birthing in May. In the delivery room, hard labor. Outside in the waiting room, the father paced.

And where had *she* been at the time? Sitting right here in this garden, torn between her anger and her love. Grace and her daughter, Elizabeth, had not spoken since before the wedding. In fact, Grace refused to even go to the wedding, claiming she was too embarrassed to be seen in public. She had not intended to see them again, either one of them.

But her heart ached with her loss. Indeed, had her only daughter been dead, she was sure it could not have hurt more. Her son-in-law sent a messenger telling her Elizabeth was in labor. And then the update about the breach position. That the doctor was concerned for both mother and baby.

But instead of rushing to the hospital to be there for her, she simply sat, alternating between resentment for the embarrassment caused her in social circles and her desire to see her first grandchild. The scent from the roses and hyacinths in full bloom were as a rare perfume, and the yellows and purples blended together in a kaleidoscope for the eyes.

How she loved the solitude of this garden. She always felt so close to God here. He seemed to be everywhere she looked.

God, how can I forgive her? How can I ask her to forgive me for being so stubborn? She really is like her father, rest his soul. Strong-willed. Determined.

She smiled as she remembered her husband saying those very words to her early in their marriage.

Maybe she is more like me than I want to admit.

She sat for some time, pondering the situation. She could choose to ignore her daughter. And never see her grandchild. Or, she could admit she was wrong to turn her back and hope her daughter would eventually forgive her.

After all, God, I know that You will never forsake me. Perhaps Elizabeth can find it in her heart to forgive this foolish old woman.

Her decision made, she gathered up a huge bouquet of purple hyacinths, the traditional flower given when saying "I'm sorry, I was wrong." Suddenly, her heart was lighter than it had been in months.

When she arrived at the hospital, she was told her daughter had already delivered and settled in her room. She walked down the long hallway, feeling somewhat like a condemned prisoner taking that final walk to the gas chamber. Her mouth was dry, and, truth be known, her knees shook. She gathered her armful of flowers closer to her chest for comfort and inhaled their heady fragrance.

She paused outside her daughter's room. Peering around the half-open door, a tender scene unfolded. Her son-in-law bent over a bundle in her daughter's arms. Her grandchild. She realized with a start that she hadn't even thought to ask if it was a boy or a girl. She shook herself—what difference did it make, really? No difference, particularly if her daughter would not forgive her.

She drew a deep breath and walked into the room. Her son-in-law turned at the sound of her footsteps on the linoleum floor. His eyebrows lifted in surprise, and her daughter looked up from the child. Grace stopped, uncertain whether to proceed or not. Not until smiles replaced their initial expressions did she know what to do. She stood beside the bed, tears streaming down her cheeks, as she offered her bouquet of flowers like a peace offering.

"Oh, Mom, they're beautiful. Hyacinths, right?"

Elizabeth buried her face deep in the blossoms. "And the wonderful smell. I'm so glad you came. Would you like to hold your granddaughter?"

Grace nodded and held out her arms to receive the child. She looked down into the tiny wrinkled face, so peaceful in sleep. This was a moment to treasure, a moment she had foolishly nearly let slip away. She was not so naive to think everything would be perfect now. Raising a family was never easy, particularly in a town filled with small minds.

But she knew her daughter. If anyone could make it, she could.

She bent to kiss the velvety soft forehead of the sleeping child in her arms. Whispering softly, she said, "Hold your head high, little girl. Be proud of who you are, and where you came from. You and I are going to have many wonderful times together. I will tell you stories of your mother when she was a little girl, just like you."

To her daughter and son-in-law, "She is beautiful. And to think I nearly missed this. I am so sorry. Can you find it in your heart to forgive me for my foolishness?"

"We already have, Mom," her son-in-law answered at once.

Grace looked from one to the other. What she saw pleased her. Complete agreement. Love for each other and for this baby.

She pushed her tears back. This wasn't a time for crying. This was a time for rejoicing. "What are you going to name this wonderful gift from God?"

Elizabeth touched her husband's hand. "We're going to name her Victoria, Tory for short. Victoria Grace."

Tory tugged on her grandmother's hand. "Nana

Grace, have you heard a word I said? You've been in some kind of a daydream."

Nana Grace reluctantly left her memories, for the moment, to come back to the present. "Yes, child, I've heard every word you said. Yellow roses, purple hyacinths. A good combination."

"Nana Grace, why don't you have hyacinths in your garden anymore? Mom says you used to be so proud of them, and they were so beautiful."

Grace paused to survey her garden once more. "You know the meaning behind purple hyacinths, don't you?" Seeing the puzzled look on her granddaughter's face, she patted her hand. "In my day, flowers were given to send a special message. Red roses for love, yellow roses for friendship, lilies for engagement. Well, purple hyacinths were to tell the recipient that you were sorry for something you had done or said. Since this is such a special day, let me tell you a story about purple hyacinths. A story about your mom and dad, and me, and you. Come, let's have another cup of coffee. We have some time…"

A Hat Like Miss Mary's

Yes, I'm an old woman full of old woman's memories and stories. And yes, sometimes I repeat myself. Can't help it. The memories and stories are so real, so vivid, it's like they happened yesterday. I see you rolling your eyes when I repeat one of my favorite tales. Not my fault. It happened yesterday or the day before, far as my mind is concerned.

But here's a story I never told you before. Let me find the page in the photo album while you pour us another cup of coffee. Careful, don't pour too fast or the lid of the pot falls into the cup, maybe breaking both. I did that once. Have I ever told you that story? I was about eight—

Oh, I already told you that one. Well, mind the lip of the pot. Don't want to chip it. That was a gift on my wedding day from my mother. Did I ever tell you about my wedding day?

Okay, fine, I'll tell you the new story. And no, I didn't just make it up, neither. Here's the page. Let me take a sip of coffee first. This old woman's throat gets dry easy.

Good. Now I can talk a bit more. You set back on that sofa right next to me. Here, let me get you a cushion. No? Fine, fine. Here's the picture. See that beautiful woman there, walking along with an armful of roses? That's Mary Elitch. She and her husband started a theater in Denver a long time ago. How long, you ask? A real long time ago. Even before I was born.

What's that? You didn't know anyone lived before I was born. Here, let me slap you. Of course people lived. Where do you think I came from? I had a mother and a father, just like you do. I had ancestors, folks who came here to Colorado when there was nothing but empty fields and giant forests. A time when the Indians roamed free, and the buffalo thundered over the plains. A time when a man could start out in the morning walking, and walk until the sun went down, and still never see another living soul.

I know, hard to believe. But in those same times, when Denver was a small town at the foot of the Rockies, John and Mary Elitch came to Denver. Mary loved the stage, and she persuaded her husband to build her a theater. He died before the theater was built, but she carried on. She brought in local actors and famous New York actors, and not-so-famous actors who became famous because they acted on her stage.

Who is the little girl in the picture? Give me a minute, child. I'm getting to it. This is my story, and I'll tell it the way I want to tell it. Mary Elitch was a lady, in the way the word 'lady' used to mean. She was gentle in spirit, fair minded, always willing to give a person a chance.

Sure, she knew which fork to use, which course to serve after the fish dish. But that's not what made her a lady.

I'll tell you what really made her a lady. She saw something in me that nobody else saw. And I believe I saw something in her nobody else saw, too.

I guess I gave it away. The little girl in the picture is me. I was about your age, ten or so, when my mother read an advertisement in the Rocky Mountain News about Elitch Theater looking for some children for an upcoming production. I loved to act and sing, and I could dance, too. Tap dance, Irish dance, square dance, you name it, I could do it. I know you wouldn't be able to tell it from these old hands and feet, so gnarled and swollen and stiff, but it's true.

So my parents talked about it, and they agreed to take me to the audition. I was certain I was going to be chosen. I wore my best dress and the cute little bonnet I'd gotten for Easter that year. As far as I was concerned, I was going to show the rest of these country bumpkins what a real actress wore.

When we got to the theater at nine the next morning, I couldn't believe how many cars and wagons and people were there. I was certain we'd made a mistake and gone to the wrong entrance. Surely these people weren't here for the audition. I begged my father to check the notice again.

But we were at the right place. There were hundreds of children with their parents, and many girls had on long gowns with crinolines, some even wore color on their eyes and their lips.

I was doomed.

Or so I thought.

We waited our turn in line. When lunch time came, Father took our car and went in search of some food for us while Mother and I continued to stand in line. All the stores in the neighborhood were sold out of most everything because of the huge crowd, and all he could find was an apple and a package of crackers. We ate like it was the best Sunday dinner, we were so hungry. When I couldn't stand any longer, my father carried me to the car and stayed with me, while my mother waited in line.

By the time our turn came, my dress was wrinkled, my hair was falling from under my bonnet, and my face was red and spotty with prickly heat. Did I mention this was in July? Ever have prickly heat? No, you don't get heat like that anymore. Why, I remember one time—

Sorry, I'll get back to my story in a minute. Need another sip of this fine joe. Do you know how long it takes to get from coffee plant to your cup? I know. Back to the story.

So there I was, standing in front of a woman, not

Mary Elitch, mind you. I'd had this thought I would get to meet Mary Elitch herself, and that she'd set eyes on me, and declare, "This is our new star. Send the rest home."

Instead, I'm standing in front of some other woman who says she's "making the cut for Miss Mary". I had to ask her what that meant. It meant she was sending home the ones who didn't get chosen.

My palms are sweaty, and I'm trying not to fidget. Mother told me not to wipe my hands in my dress because my hands were dirty, and they're itching, and I've got prickly heat on my face and arms, and I've really got to go to the bathroom, because we've been waiting since early, and now it's after lunch. And this woman looks me over, up and down, like I'm a calf at a 4-H auction. Her lips pucker up, her eyes go all squinty, and she starts to shake her head.

The room goes black around me, and the next thing I know, I'm laying on a bench outside under the shade of a huge tree, and an angel is sitting beside me, wiping my face with something cool and wet. I look up at her, and she smiles at me, and I see heaven dance in her eyes.

I tried to sit up, and she puts a soft white hand on my shoulder and presses me back onto the bench. "Just stay still another moment." Her voice is like a creek bubbling over the rocks, all sweet and full of life. "Have another drink."

I look over her shoulder to where Mother and my father are standing. Mother is wringing her hands, and my father has his arm around Mother's shoulders. It's nice to see them standing close like that. He doesn't do that often, at least not where I can see it.

But back to the angel who is sitting next to me. She holds a glass in her hand, and the glass is covered with frost, and water drips down the side, and suddenly I'm so thirsty, like my tongue is swollen up and filling my mouth, threatening to choke me. She slips one arm under my head, and raises me up. I reach for the glass, and she tips it ever so slightly until some of the liquid runs past my lips.

Overwhelming cold and sweet and tart fill my mouth. Lemonade of the best kind. Bits of pulp touch my tongue, and I swallow. It's so cold it feels like a huge lump moving down my throat. I cough once, and she lets up on the glass. I reach for the glass with my hands, and I touched her hand. The skin was as soft as a kitten's nose, and there weren't any calluses or dry skin I could see.

She lets me drink that whole glass all by myself, but she makes me do it slowly. Said something about not gulping it too fast or I might get a tummy ache. Like I said, a lady.

Once I drank it all, I started to feel a little better, so she helped me sit up. Then she told the first woman who didn't seem to like the looks of me to take my parents inside and get them something cold to drink. "I want to take a walk with this young lady," she said.

"Yes, Miss Mary," the woman said.

My ministering angel was Miss Mary Elitch.

Miss Mary reached past me to a table and picked up a large summer hat, then stood as she pinned the hat to her hair. Holding out a hand to me, which I took, she led me down the path, through the gardens full of statues and trees and flowers. All the while, she chatted to me like I had sense, not like I was a child of ten. She pointed out some of the famous people statues, like Shakespeare, Frost, Browning. She asked what I liked to read, and I admitted I didn't really like to read.

She stopped and turned to me, her hands on my shoulders, a real serious look on her face. "If you want to succeed in life, you must love reading. Read anything you can get your hands on, even if you don't understand it.

Read package labels, street signs, menus, newspapers. Do you understand?"

I didn't really, but I nodded.

She nodded and smiled at me, her sweet angel smile.

I would have said or done anything to have her smile at me.

So we continued walking and talking. She asked me what I liked to do, what was my favorite subject in school, all kinds of things. Most people don't think a ten-year-old girl knows very much, but she didn't act that way. She treated me like a real person.

While we walked, I kept looking up into her face, watching her smile, frown, grimace, laugh. I wanted to know how a lady showed every emotion. I wanted to see into her soul if I could, so I could remember this day forever.

Second Chances and Second Cups

Let's take a break now so I can have more coffee. I know you want to hear the rest of the story, but I'm an old woman, and I need to catch my breath, let my memories catch up with my talking. Good, you poured that very well. Not too quickly. No tapping of the pot against the rim of the cup. Settle down, now, and I'll finish my story.

So there we were, walking and talking and just enjoying each other's company. At least, I was enjoying her company, and I believe she was enjoying mine. And all the while, that marvelous hat of hers is keeping the sun off her face, shading her from the burning rays of the sun. And my simple bonnet that doesn't have a rim is making my head hot, and I want to rip the bonnet off and let it hang by its strings down my back, but I daren't, because by that time I just knew my hair was such a mess.

I kept tucking stray ends of hair underneath my bonnet, and fidgeting with the strings, loosening them and flicking them out of the way. The bonnet made me feel like such a baby. Before I met Miss Mary, I thought I was so classy, and now having her here by my side just makes me feel silly.

We pass the rose garden, and Miss Mary wants to stop and look at the flowers. The place smells so pretty, and there are colors of roses I never seen before. I knew about red roses and white roses, and once I even read a story about yellow roses, but she had about ten different kinds of pink roses, and some that were red and white, and yellow and pink. Some of the roses were so tiny, and some were bigger than my hand.

She picked up a pair of shears and put on a pair of gloves. "Will you help me choose some blossoms for a bouquet for my dining room table?"

I don't know why she thought I knew anything about roses, but I nodded. I would have helped her dig a ditch if she'd asked me to, then filled it again just because it pleased her. We spent a long time choosing roses. She'd cut one, then hold it up to another to see if it looked nice together. When she'd cut about a dozen roses, she set them aside and turned to me.

"Would you like to choose some roses for your mother?"

Flowers for Mother? What a thought. I couldn't remember my mother ever having fresh flowers in our home. She grew some flowers, just common ones, though, like phlox and mums and pansies. Nothing so fancy as roses.

I didn't know whether Mother would like some roses, but I certainly would. I nodded, feeling only a little pang of guilt at the deceit. I would offer them to Mother first, and if she didn't want them, then it would be fine to keep them. At least, that was my thinking.

So we chose another dozen of the most beautiful roses I'd ever seen. I thought they were even nicer than the one Miss Mary chose for her table. She showed me how to carry them so the thorns wouldn't prick me, then she gathered her roses and we walked back toward the theater.

I was sorry our time together was coming to an end, and so I kind of dragged my feet. Miss Mary saw I wasn't hurrying to get back, so we stopped on a bench and talked some more.

"Have you had a good time here today?"

I nodded. "I sure have. I came for the audition, and I ended up spending time with you. This is like a dream come true for me."

She smiled, and I noticed a small dimple in her cheek. I wanted a dimple like that.

"Then why are you sad?"

"Because I won't see you again. That lady didn't

like me. She was shaking her head. I think that's why I fainted."

Miss Mary began to laugh, a quiet, polite laugh that soon erupted from inside her and overtook her. She leaned back on the bench and held her tummy with her hands. In fact, she leaned back so far her hat fell off.

I jumped up, scampered around the bench, and picked up her hat. My hands were full of roses, so all I could do was stand there, her hat in my hand, roses pricking at my arms, and watch her laugh. I knew she was having a good time, but I didn't understand why. My face went all hot because I thought she was laughing at me. I didn't like that very much. It was all bad enough that my time with her was over, but she didn't need to laugh at me.

After a long while, Miss Mary stopped laughing. She pulled a handkerchief from up her sleeve and dabbed at her eyes, ever so delicately so as to not smear her makeup. She patted the bench beside her, and I sat down.

"Why is your mouth turned down?"

I wouldn't look at her. "You were laughing at me."

She pulled me close into her arms, and I smelled her perfume, lilac, I think. It reminded me of warm summer days and clean laundry on a clothesline. I snuggled closer, wanting not to be mad at her.

"I wasn't laughing at you. I was laughing at what you said. There is a difference."

I pulled back and stared into her eyes. My father said a person's eyes were the window to their soul. I wanted to see what her soul was really saying. "What difference?"

She spread her arms wide. "A huge difference." She dropped her arms. "That woman, who is my assistant, wasn't shaking her head because she was going to send you home. She was shaking her head because she couldn't believe her eyes."

I tilted my head to one side. I was confused.

"We were looking for some children to take on various parts in our plays."

I nodded. This much I knew.

"And, we were looking for someone to play one particular ten-year-old girl." She paused. "We are going to do a play about my life, and we needed someone to play me when I was ten. She couldn't believe how much you look like I did when I was your age."

She thought I looked like her? But she was a beautiful woman, a lady, successful. And I was—

Miss Mary lifted her hat from my hands and brushed the dust and grass off, careful not to dislodge the flowers and ribbons that decorated the crown. She loosened the strings of my bonnet, slipped the clumsy thing off my head and down my back, where it hung by the ribbons at my throat. Then she set her hat on my head, tucking some strands of hair behind my ears. We both laughed because the hat was too big for me and covered my eyes so I couldn't see. She took her hat back and pinned it back to her hair.

Standing, she shifted her roses in her arms. "Let's go back and talk to your parents. We need their permission if you are going to play the part."

We walked back to the theater, our relationship repaired. We chatted about the play, and practice times, and how I needed to keep up my grades in school, and learn the script if I wanted to be an actress.

And I did want to be an actress. I wanted to be everything Miss Mary was. Over the coming years, I worked hard at school, acted in many plays with Miss Mary, and even traveled around the world with her.

Now that I'm an old woman, I don't act anymore.

Mostly I just sit here with my memories. Sometimes I help out at the theater. This year they are renovating the old Elitch Theater. They want to put on productions just like they did in the old days.

Of course, Miss Mary won't be there. She's been gone for a long time now. But when we reopen the theater, we are going to do the same play Miss Mary chose me to do with her, the story of her life. I'm going to play her as an old woman, and we'd like you to play her as a ten-year-old girl. Would you like that?

I knew you would. I knew you were the one to do it, the one to bring Miss Mary to life again on the stage. I saw her in your eyes the first time I met you.

What will you be paid? Of course, you young people today, that's what you want to know, isn't it? Well, you'll get exactly what I got when I played the part so many years ago.

Let me get it for you. It's over here in this closet. Oh, my aching back. Sometimes I think sitting so long is what makes me stiff. I'll be glad to get back to work on this play. Here it is.

Do you like it? It's my most treasured possession. Miss Mary gave me this to wear in the play, and I'm going to give it to you.

It's a hat just like Miss Mary's. Just like the one in this picture.

It's a lady's hat.

Oh, yes, it's too big for you yet. Just like it was too big for me.

But it will work fine. And you will work fine.

Now, pour us some more coffee. No, more milk in yours. You might be an actress, but you're still a child.

But someday you, too, will be a lady.

Second Chances and Second Cups

Satin & Ruffles

"Oh, Gramma..." That's as far as Kayla could get before her voice broke.

Her mother and grandmother beamed at her, the tears in their eyes threatening to spill over.

Her mother spoke first. "See, Mom, I told you she would love it."

Kayla stared at the monstrosity before her, unable to believe this was happening.

This was not the way it was supposed to be. In her mind's eye, Kayla had seen her prom dress, and how she would look wearing it, for at least a year now. Never mind that she had changed her mind several times about the color. Not wanting to wear the same color as any of the other girls, she had waited until they had all chosen their dresses. There was really only one place in town to buy such a dress, Sally's Prom and Bridal Shoppe. A very pretentious name for what was really just a converted garage in Sally's house. McGregor's Department Store surely wouldn't carry a suitable gown for such a momentous occasion. It wasn't every day a girl graduated high school, was it?

No indeed. And such a celebration warranted no ordinary dress. The only dress truly suitable was the ivory tea-length satin Kayla had set aside months ago. Once she confirmed it was the only dress like it in town, and that all the other girls were choosing pastel shades of blue or pink, Kayla knew the gown was hers. She scrimped and saved until she had the fifty dollars Sally wanted to hold the dress, and she managed to get enough babysitting jobs to make the installment payments Sally insisted on to make sure she still wanted the dress. And she did.

At least, up until today. No, that wasn't quite true. She still wanted the dress. More than she wanted anything in all her life. But today, her mother and grandmother surprised her with this—this pale imitation of a gown. Where the one Kayla wanted was the color of homemade vanilla ice cream, this one was green. Peppermint green.

And instead of the simple bodice covered with hand-sewn pearls, this one was ruffles up and down and all around. And what was it with the dead flowers on the sleeves?

Kayla was speechless. Her mother and grandmother sat on the edge of her bed, waiting for her to continue. Tears filled Kayla's eyes, and try as she might she could not contain them They slipped down her cheeks in silent rivers, dripping on the dress.

"Mother made that for my prom," her mother said. "I felt like a fairy princess. And I thought that since the styles don't change much, and Mother had put so much work into the dress, it was such a waste to only use it once. I think if we let down the hem some, and take it in at the waist, it will be perfect. What do you think, Kayla?"

Kayla couldn't find the words to express what she truly thought. Her mother's prom dress? It had to be nearly twenty years old! And styles surely did change. She didn't want to hurt either one of them, but she also didn't want to be seen in public in this dress. She looked at her grandmother, willing herself to smile.

When she focused on her Gramma's face, she knew her Gramma knew. The relationship Kayla had with her grandmother was almost magical. Sometimes it was as if they could read each other's minds, without even speaking. Even now, in these turbulent teenage years, Kayla's Gramma was her confidante, her best friend. The only secret that Kayla had ever kept from her Gramma was the prom dress.

"Why don't you leave us girls alone for a bit while we try on this gown and get it fitted?" Her Gramma ushered Kayla's mother to the door. "Maybe put on a pot of coffee. I cold use something to drink."

"Okay. Coffee sounds good. I'll bring it in when it's ready." She gave Kayla a quick hug. "Oh, I'm so excited to see you in this dress."

Gramma closed the bedroom door. "Kayla, what's going on? You can't fool me, you know."

"Nothing's going on, Gramma. I was just surprised that Momma would want to share her dress with me, knowing it would have to be altered. You know how

Momma is about saving things like this. Why, she once told me that she wouldn't even let me borrow her wedding dress when I get married. Why should this dress be any different?"

"Can I tell you a secret?" her Gramma leaned in close, even though the door was closed. "Promise you won't say a word to anyone?"

"Promise."

"Your momma never wore this dress." Seeing the look on Kayla's face, she went on quickly. "Oh, I know, she talks like she did. But she didn't. She kinda got stood up that night. The boy who was supposed to take her got called into the service right before the dance, and everyone else already had their date. She was so embarrassed, she didn't show her face outside of her room for two weeks! I kept trying to tell her that it wasn't the end of the world, but for her, at that time, it was. Your momma designed the dress, you know."

"I didn't know that. Momma hates sewing."

"Yes, she hates sewing, but she loved designing

clothes. She took some art classes in school, applied to a couple of design schools. But she lost interest when she didn't get to go to the prom. She married the first man that came along after that, and you were born a year later."

"I didn't know all that about Momma. I always thought she wanted to be a mother and a wife. She seemed so happy and so good at it. And I know she loves Daddy"

"She does, don't get me wrong. It's just that on the way, she had some heartache. The boy who was s'posed to take her to the prom? He never came home again. Died in some foreign place we never heard of before. Doesn't seem right, somehow." Her Gramma's voice trailed off. "So many dreams died that night."

"Gramma, does Momma ever talk about the prom she never got to go to?"

"Child, she has been so excited about you getting to go this year that I don't know how you could have missed it in her." Gramma smiled. "Or maybe you've both been keeping secrets?"

Kayla realized she'd been caught, and told her

about the dress she had on hold. Gramma agreed that was the dress that was perfect for Kayla, just as this dress had been perfect for her mother.

"Gramma, I've got an idea, but I need to make some phone calls first. I'll be back in a few minutes."

With that, Kayla fairly flew from the room, down to the telephone in the kitchen. Less than ten minutes later, she came back into the bedroom, where her Gramma was still sitting on the bed, fingering the material and the ruffles on the dress. "Everything is set. Momma is going to the prom, even if she did have to wait all this time! Daddy will be her date, and he's going to rent a limousine and everything! Won't that be great?"

"Won't what be great?" Her mother came into the room bearing a tray with three coffee cups. "Are you two still in here, mooning over this dress?"

"Momma, how do you feel about going to a prom?"

Her mother shot a quick glance at Gramma, who had the good grace to blush.

"What stories have you been telling this child?"

"This child, as you call her, practically forced me to tell her the story of how you never got to wear this lovely dress." Kayla's Gramma declared. "I'm lucky to be alive, considering all the torture she put me through." She added, with a laugh. "Okay, so don't believe a word I'm saying. Anyway, she asked you a question. Are you going or not? Might be your one and only chance to dance the night away in this designer original gown."

Kayla's mother looked from one to the other. "I don't stand a chance when the two of you gang up on me. Don't tell me I have a choice. I'd never hear the end of it if I didn't go and keep an eye on my little friend here. Come on, ladies—we've got a prom to plan for!" She gestured to the tray. "But first, let's drink our coffee before it gets cold."

The Sun Through the Clouds

The taxi pulled up, deposited its cargo, and left. His fare, fourteen-year-old Margaret, just stood there, clutching a worn denim purse to her chest as she stared at the house. An older woman watching from the front window rapped on the glass, bidding her to come in. Margaret picked up her small backpack, shrugged, and proceeded up the walkway. Anything had to be better than juvenile hall, even living with a grandmother she'd never met. After all, how bad could it be, living with an old woman?

Her grandmother opened the front door as the child walked slowly towards her. This was not a meeting Margaret had looked forward to, and, in fact, it would never have happened if her mother had taken her responsibility seriously. Then again, as a single parent she did have to work to support the two of them.

The old lady eyed her up and down as if she was specimen on the end of a pin under a glass case. "Hello. You must be Margaret. You may call me Grandmother. I won't abide with any familiarities like Gram. Is that clear?" Her voice was strong, and she spoke as though she was used to being obeyed.

"Yes, ma'am. I mean Grandmother." Margaret replied.

Grandmother smiled. "You seem well-trained. I'd expected a little more fire, considering who her mother was."

If she's going to badmouth my mother—Margaret sighed and held her tongue. Three months should pass fast enough.

"Come in, and I'll show you your room. You will keep it tidy, change your own sheets, do your own laundry, and keep your bathroom clean. Anything you break will come directly from your own money...." Her voice trailed off as she walked down the hallway and paused outside a closed door.

Margaret stood rooted to her spot in the open doorway. This woman sounded more like a drill sergeant than a grandmother. Not that she had much experience with grandmothers. Or mothers, for that matter.

The woman turned to face her. "Where are you, child? Don't dawdle. We have things to do. This house doesn't revolve around you, you know."

Margaret crossed her arms over her chest and stuck out her chin. "Look, I don't know what you're trying to prove with this mightier-than-thou act. The court said I have a choice, here or Juvy. I chose here, because it seemed like a better place to be. Now I'm not sure I made the right choice." Margaret drew herself up to her full height and put her hands on her hips.

"I see there is some fight left in you." She turned toward the closed door again. "You made the right choice. Juvy, as you call it, would have made you worse. By the time you leave here, you'll be thanking me. You'll see."

The next weeks went by quickly. Most days were spent in quiet solitude in the garden. The grandmother loved the garden, pulling a dead leaf here, straightening a stake there. Her gardener came in to do the heavy work, but she delighted in tending to the flowers herself. She wore a large straw hat to keep the sun off her face and shoulders. The day Margaret came out clad in a tiny two-piece swim suit, Grandmother was outraged. She made her go back in and change. After all, 'only field hands and laborers get suntans' was her belief.

On one occasion when she insisted that Margaret help her weed the garden, she made a very pointed remark to her granddaughter. "If you don't get rid of them, weeds will choke out even the strongest."

To which Margaret replied, after a moment's consideration, "Sometimes it can be difficult to tell the weeds from the rest, don't you think, Grandmother?"

Another day, when Margaret's back was tired from bending over the flowerbeds and her knees were sore, she snapped at the older woman, "Why do you do this when you can afford to hire someone to do it for you?"

Her grandmother pinched off another dead flower head. "Some labors of love are best done yourself."

Margaret wasn't sure what she was getting at, so she stayed silent.

And so they spent their days, more or less in silence, as if they lived alone. Each in their own world, untouched by the other, day to day in the same house but not in the same world.

The only bright spot in Margaret's life was their weekly visits to the library. They walked there every Monday, as it was Grandmother's belief that most people returned their books on Saturday, so the best selection was to be had on Mondays. Margaret loved to read romantic history stories, totally immersing herself in the make-believe world of the past, where everyone lived happily ever after. Grandmother said it was a lot of drivel and encouraged her to broaden her interests by reading other types of stories. But Margaret couldn't get past the first page or two before she put it aside.

On one trip to the library, Grandmother selected a book for Margaret that had a number of short romance stories with flowers as their theme. When she showed it to her, Margaret forced a smile.

"Thank you, Grandmother. I appreciate you thinking of me." she said politely, fully intending to return the book unread. But on Saturday, having read all her other books, she leafed through the book and found, to her surprise, that she enjoyed the style of writing and the characters. She read it from cover to cover, and then she read it again. The stories touched a part of her heart that she hadn't felt before, that place that whispered that life could be good. That there was hope for the future. She liked that feeling.

She went in search of her grandmother and found her in the garden, bent over a small bush. The sky was clouding over, and it looked like it would rain soon.

Walking up to the elderly woman, Margaret laid her hand on her grandmother's shoulder. This was the first time either had touched the other. "Grandmother, thank you for choosing this book for me. I really enjoyed it.".

"I'm glad. It was one of my favorites when I was your age."

Margaret smiled. "Really? So we have something in common."

"I guess we do, child. You know, my garden is like therapy for me. My husband, your grandfather, died when your father was very young. He left us well provided for, so I never had to work. Not that I could have gotten a job anyway. Women weren't trained to work outside of the home in those days."

"I didn't know that, Grandmother."

"Then when your father went away, my world fell apart. My whole life had been about him, you see. I know I spoiled him. He never did a day's work before he married your mother." Grandmother's eyes filled with tears. "After he left, the only thing that got me through was this garden. And God."

Margaret huffed into her bangs. "Don't start on me about church and stuff, because I don't believe in that. My mom says that God is for weak people who can't stand on their own two feet." Margaret took her hand from her grandmother's shoulder and stepped back, putting some distance between her and this weird old woman.

"I can understand that. She needed to be strong for your father, and more so when he left. But maybe if she hadn't been quite so strong, he might not have—" Grandmother left the suggestion hanging there.

She didn't need to finish. Margaret had heard it often enough from neighbors, teachers, even her own mother had once said the same thing.

Her grandmother continued. "I was strong then, too. Much stronger than I am now. I know I made him like he was. If I'd raised him different, maybe he wouldn't have left."

"Now that's different. The grown-ups taking the blame. I thought that was our job as kids—to blame our parents for our mistakes." Margaret chuckled at the turn of the tables.

"Put blame where blame is due, I always say. But Margaret," Grandmother's tone was more serious now. "I meant what I said about God getting me through the hard times. I remember one time I came here to this very garden. I was so depressed, I wanted to end it all."

Margaret knew how her grandmother felt. She'd had a lot of days when she'd felt the same way. Only she didn't have a garden to go to. Or a God who would listen.

God didn't listen to girls like her.

Her grandmother continued. "I was kneeling here and crying out to God. 'God, I can't live like this. I need to know You still love me.' It was a dark, overcast day, just like my mood. And in an instant, the sun broke through the clouds, and the sunbeams shone down, like rays of gold. And I was reminded of something *my* grandmother used to say. 'When you see the sun rays shining through the clouds, that's God's love shining on you.' And I knew He loved me, and would always be there for me."

"Well, that's a nice story, and I'm sure you believe that, but not me. God doesn't love me. He couldn't. Not after the things I've done. If He loved me, my dad would be here, and we would all be together."

"God doesn't always plan things the way we would, child. But He always knows what's best."

Margaret shook her head, her pony tail slapping her in the cheeks. "Then this God of yours needs to prove it to me."

The words were hardly out of her mouth when there was a loud clap of thunder, and lightning bolts danced along the horizon. But rather than rain, the sun broke through the clouds and filled the sky with the most glorious arrangement of sun rays, piercing the dark sky and lighting His world.

Piercing one child's dark heart, lighting her life.

And reminding His much older child that His love for her was still true and real.

Coming of Age

The mountains to the west shone brightly as the first rays of the morning sun hit them. Upstairs in her room, Laurie snuggled under the goose down quilt, not at all anxious to set her feet on the cold floor. Downstairs, her mother moved around the small kitchen as she prepared breakfast. Her father came in the back door and dumped an armful of wood in the wood box.

"Laurie, breakfast will be ready in five minutes." her mother called out. "And it's your favorite—bacon and eggs."

Bacon and eggs? On a weekday? Something strange here. Usually she had hot oatmeal on weekday mornings. For as long as she could remember, bacon and eggs were special, saved for Sunday morning. And why was her mother getting her out of bed so early, when she knew Laurie didn't have classes at the community college until this afternoon? *Parents. Who could figure them out?*

Laurie hopped out of bed and got into her clothes as quick as she could. Which wasn't real quick, given she couldn't decide if today was a pink day or a blue day. After trying on two pairs of jeans—why had she bought the pair that made her hips look as wide as a barn door—and three shirts, she finally settled for blue jeans and a pink shirt. At the head of the stairs, she called down to her mother, "Going to the bathroom and I'll be right down."

Her father's voice followed her into the small bathroom the whole family shared. "You'd best be quick about it. Eggs are almost done."

Brush her teeth, wash her face, a perfunctory swipe at her short curly hair. Golly, she couldn't imagine spending the time on her hair that some of the girls in class did. Good thing she wasn't going out for beautician, or she'd have to spend time on that stuff.

Un-unh—none of that foolishness for her. She was being sensible, as her father said, and learning a real trade —secretarial. The classes were boring, but she was sure to get a job at the factory where her dad worked when she graduated. And that was really important. In a small town, where there weren't many jobs, getting a factory job was practically a guarantee of success. Several of her older cousins had gone to work at the factory and met their husbands-to-be there. Then they got married, and didn't have to work anymore.

That was Laurie's prayer. She wanted to be married and have children, and a house of her own, and a picket fence, and, and. . .

She sighed. Already wishing her life away. She applied a little mascara—her parents complained if she dolled herself up too much—a quick toilet stop, then she clattered down the stairs. The smell of perking coffee on the stove teased her as she reached the bottom and rounded the corner. Like a carrot held out of reach, every morning she woke to the smell of freshly perked coffee. Whenever she smelled the hot beverage, she thought of home and family. Although she had never tasted it, she just knew that she would like it. Her parents had been very strict about her not having coffee 'until she was old enough'.

Just what did that mean, anyway? Old enough for what? She already had her driver's license, and next year she would be able to vote. She was in her first year of community college, practically grown up. When would her parents loosen the apron strings and treat her more like an adult?

She went downstairs and paused in the doorway of the kitchen to drink in the wonderful smells. Bacon, fresh bread, and, of course, coffee. This was a wonderful old house. Her parents had lived here since before Laurie was born. It was a company house, belonging to the factory, but it was so familiar it felt like they owned it. Her mom had painted some of the rooms, and even put wallpaper in the front entryway. Her dad sat, his elbows on the table, his plate untouched in front of him. Her mother was bustling at something on the stove. A bit too bustling, like she was trying to keep busy. *God, don't let there be anything wrong.*

"Good morning, Mom and Dad." Her voice sounded shrill, like she was trying to be happy when she wasn't. And she had no reason not to be happy. Did she?

Maybe she did. Her parents were sure acting strange this morning. She couldn't remember the last time her dad put his elbows on the table and her mother hadn't tsk-tsked at him until he sat up straight. *Mothers.*

And usually Dad was already gone to the plant by the time she crawled down the stairs around ten. She liked to sleep in and had arranged her classes for later in the day.

Not to mention the early call, and the whole cooked breakfast thing.

Had the body snatchers come and grabbed her parents during the night?

No, that was just in the movies.

"Good morning, sweetheart." Her mother still wouldn't look at her. "I hope you're hungry. You're dad's appetite seems to have flown south with the birds today." *Boy, does she sound fake..*

"Sit down, Laurie, we got some talking to do." Her father's voice, always such a comfort to her, now sounded sad and worn out. Her dad had always been strong, decisive. Sometimes a little hard, but she had never been afraid of him.

Now she didn't want to hear what would come next.

"Pour her a cup of coffee, Elizabeth. She's come of age today."

Come of age? Today? What was going on? It wasn't her birthday. Was she in trouble for something? Laurie could not remember one thing she had done that would warrant this kind of seriousness. Was someone sick? Did Grandpa die? What could be this bad, this early in the day? *O God, not Grandpa, not bad news, please.*

Laurie stared at the cup of coffee in front of her as if it were something alien. She was afraid to drink it. She felt like Alice in Wonderland. Once she drank that coffee, nothing would ever be the same again. She just knew it. "What's going on, Dad? Mom?"

"Your dad has something to tell you, honey." Her mother's eyes met her father's across the table. Unspoken emotion flowed between them.

Second Chances and Second Cups

This was serious.

Her father took a deep breath and began, "The factory is closing down. We got a month to move out of here. Your mom and me have prayed about this a lot. We gotta move somewhere else and find a place to live and another job for me. Laurie, you'll have to quit school, at least for now, and find a job in the new place we move. I think we'll go to a big city, where there are lots of factories, and lots of jobs. I know I'll have to start at the bottom again, and so probably won't be able to get you a job like I had kinda promised. . . " His voice trailed off, and he stared out the window.

The factory closing? They had to move? No job for her? No job meant no husband, no kids, no dream. Laurie fought to hold back her tears. She stared at the coffee in front of her, and she lost the battle. Her tears dripped into the fragrant black liquid, creating little ripples on the surface. Ripples like on a pond when you throw in a stone.

And that reminded her of a Scripture verse she had read during her devotion time the previous evening: "You are like living stones being built into a ...holy priesthood". That meant God must have a reason for all that He was doing. And although she felt like her whole world was slipping away, like her dreams didn't mean anything, she knew it wasn't all about her.

Because what about her dad and his dreams? He longed to provide for his family, and to retire and spend time in the garden with her mother. They hadn't ever had a real vacation and she knew he secretly wanted to take her mother on a cruise for their twenty-fifth anniversary. He had been saving his overtime in an old coffee can in the woodshed for years. Once he had shown her some cruise line brochures. It was their secret, just the two of them, and it made her feel grown up.

Now her dad was past fifty, and he really didn't know how to do anything except the job he had in the factory. Would he be able to find another job somewhere else? If he couldn't, she would have to support the three of them. Then what? How likely was it that she would meet a man who would want to support her, her kids-to-be, and her parents? Laurie felt like dying. She prayed that a big hole would open up and swallow her, right there, on the spot.

But what was it her father had said? "She's come of age today." Her mother and father expected her to act like a grown-up, and she wasn't about to let them down. God said that with Him, all things are possible. Laurie gulped, swiped away her tears, and put on a brave smile as she looked at her parents.

"We are going to be okay. After all, we're family, and family sticks together. We'll do just fine." She sipped her coffee. Her first cup of coffee. She was grown up. She was mature enough to handle whatever happened. After all, she wasn't alone. There were her parents, and, of course, God, to support her, strengthen her, and direct her paths.

"And this is the best coffee I've ever tasted." She smiled, and a chuckle rose from deep inside her. Yes, everything was going to be okay. Sure, there were bound to be some hard times. Some hurdles to overcome. But together, they could get through.

Second Chances and Second Cups

Ten Fingers and Ten Toes

It had been a difficult delivery, made the more so because of her fears and doubts. In 1937, unwed motherhood was not encouraged. People counted backwards on their fingers from the baby's birth date to the wedding date. In this case, there was no doubt. Married in January, birthing in May. She'd been in hard labor since yesterday morning, and she wasn't sure how much more she could endure. And it wasn't just the contractions that were wearing her down. She saw the faces of the nurses behind the masks. She heard the voices of her mother and grandmother out in the waiting room. She wished her love could be with her. For her, theirs was a forever kind of love. They'd had so little time to be alone together since the wedding. One moment of fleshly weakness had completely changed their lives. Already engaged, already promised to each other. And now they would pay for that one mistake forever, in the nasty whispers, the shame of everyone knowing what they had done.

It had taken several months to understand that her greatest fears were about to be realized. And the greatest fears of her mother, of her own entire generation. Surely pre-marital sex wasn't unique to her generation, but to hear them talk, you would think it was unheard of before. Another thing not invented by her generation were the predictions whispered around parlors and across hymnals. Tales of deformed babies born to unwed mothers, tales of deafness as punishment for a mother who would not listen as a child, reports of blindness to repay prying eyes. Every birth defect explained by a sin in the parent's life.

She sought solace in God's word, but found no sure

answer. Some scriptures said God would punish the sins of the fathers to the fourth generation. One scripture said that the man born blind was not because of sin, but to show the glory of God. She'd been too ashamed to ask their pastor. His pious and self-righteous attitude scared her, and the very fact he'd refused to perform their marriage ceremony was sentence enough for her. And so she'd gone directly to God. Having confessed her sin to Him, she pleaded with Him for the life of her unborn child. And He had answered with a husband, a home, and the promise that He would be with her, through all things.

She overheard snatches of conversation from the attending physician and the nurses. Her eyes drooped from the chloroform administered to ease the pain. Maybe this was simply a bad dream. Maybe if she forced her eyes open, she would wake up in the tiny attic bedroom she shared with her younger sister. Wasn't this Saturday?

Surely she was supposed to get dressed. They were heading out to a barn dance that evening in the new dress her mother had made for her. In the deep ragged crevices of her heart, she knew that wasn't going to happen. This was her life now; this was her baby.

Her baby. Hers. Hers and her love's. Would they live happily ever after, like in the fairy tales? It certainly didn't seem so, not looking at where they were now. Living in two rooms, orange crates for tables, a thin mattress on the floor. If this is what married life was supposed to be, she didn't see any rainbow. There had been no dowry from her father except the sharp side of his tongue. No gifts such as other brides received. On top of that, her love had been unwell for the past several months and hadn't worked much. Times were hard enough without having to compete for too few jobs with too many able-bodied men.

Given her condition, she hadn't been able to hold

her position as a teacher at the small multi-grade school. Pregnancy was not a thing to be flaunted. Church was fine, and even some simple shopping. But definitely not working, particularly teaching. Heaven forbid that the children should be exposed to the results of activities that went on behind closed doors. And, of course, they were just as able to count backwards on their fingers, having learned ably from their parents.

What was the doctor saying? Push! Push? She hardly had enough energy to breathe, let alone push. She struggled to summon enough strength to do as she was told. A weight pressed on her abdomen, and her insides, her private parts, felt like they were going to rip apart. And just as quickly, the pressure was gone. Her head fell back to the pillow, sweat mingling with tears on her cheeks.

She listened. What was that? A baby's cry? Her baby was alive, not dead, as her grandmother had

Second Chances and Second Cups

predicted. She couldn't see what was going on beyond her draped knees, ankles tied in place to keep her in position on the birthing table.

"Give me my baby." Her lips dry and parched from hours of effort and no water stumbled over the words. "I want to see my baby."

"We have to clean her up." The uppity nurse with the pinched lips and sour breath frowned at her.

"Give me my baby now!" Her insistence paid off, and a squirming bundle was pressed into her waiting arms.

She blinked in the yellow light of the delivery room and gazed into the tiny face, all wrinkled, still bloody. She checked under the swaddling cloth. A girl. Dark blue eyes stared up at her, and then the whole face wrinkled into one big squall. Her baby, a beautiful girl. Somehow she hadn't expected blue eyes. Her eyes and her loves eyes were brown. A strong, health cry came from the infant. How could something so small make such a loud noise?

"Her eyes will change color in a few weeks." Another nurse, one with a kindly smile, busied herself nearby, untying her ankles, adding another blanket across her bed. "All babies are born with blue eyes. A little startling, isn't it? I think she's probably hungry."

She nodded mutely, so overwhelmed with emotion she couldn't speak. She carefully unwrapped her baby and painstakingly counted her fingers. Five on each hand. Ten perfect fingers, stretching and clutching in the cool air. Next the toes. Five and five. Ten. She counted them again. The same.

She pulled the baby to her breast, and the child began to suckle instantly. She settled back to nurse her, oblivious to what was going on around her. Suddenly she was at peace. While all around her was involved in the activities following a successful birthing, she marveled at the child at her breast, vigorously feeding, tiny fingers moving in rhythm with her suckling.

She vaguely heard a nurse go to the waiting room to announce the birth. "It's a girl, healthy, six pounds and four ounces."

From the waiting room came cries of "Praise the Lord, a healthy baby", and "I told you she would be all right". The women of her family and her in-laws arguing over who had been right and who was wrong about predicted defects in the baby.

Her love came into the room, allowed at last to be present at the culmination of an act where only he and she had been present in the beginning. She'd been worried he had married her only to give her baby a name, to do the right thing, and that perhaps he would leave her soon after.

But when she saw the look of love on his face, the relief and joy that she had come safely through this, bringing such a beautiful part of her with her, she knew—he was here. For life.

"Ten fingers and ten toes." She whispered. "Her name is Elizabeth. Don't you think she looks like an Elizabeth?"

He nodded and tenderly touched her cheek with his forefinger, as if afraid she would break. He bent low over her, and kissed her cracked lips first, and then planted his lips on the crown of their daughter's head. "She does look like an Elizabeth."

"They were all wrong, my love, she is perfect. Ten fingers and ten toes."

He nodded. "A perfect gift from God."

She smiled. Her husband, her child, and God.

Perfect, indeed.

New Beginnings

"Got any spare change?" The unkempt young woman blocked my path, her jeans tattered at the heels, her hair at least six months past a cut. I had more important places to be than here on the street, on a cold and blustery morning in downtown Chicago.

"Um, no change." That was always my reaction. Close them out, ignore them. Just another bum on the street.

Then my eyes met hers, and something tugged at my heart.

"I was just going to get a cup of coffee. Would you join me?" I heard myself asking. What was happening here? Just moments before, I had no intention of going for coffee. I was a woman on a mission.

"Me? You want to have coffee with me?" She seemed truly amazed that I spoke to her.

"Sure. Nothing fancy. Just a little coffee shop I know." I still wasn't sure that this was a good idea, but the invitation was already given, and no matter what else people said about me, I never renege on an invitation.

"Well..." She looked as unsure as I felt.

I smiled at her, a genuine one this time. "Come on. I need a break and you need to warm up. I'll even buy you a slice of pie."

"Pie? You're on!" She grabbed her backpack from the ground at her feet and turned to follow me.

We found a table for two in the café I remembered from around the corner. It wasn't a place I normally frequented, but then again, this wasn't exactly a situation where I wanted to be seen by anyone I knew. The waitress came to the table, warily eyeing the beggar, her glance going from one to the other of us, trying to figure out the connection.

I ignored the menus she set before us. "Two coffees, and, what's the pie of the day?"

"We got coconut cream, apple, lemon meringue, and cherry." Her weary reply sounded rehearsed and stale. Hopefully the food was fresh. Then she smiled and leaned closer. "But the coconut cream is the best."

"I'll have the coconut cream, and my friend here will have?" I looked to the young woman for her order.

Now that I actually looked at her, I saw she was more of a girl than a woman. But there was an aging, a tiredness, that tainted her youth in some way. Too-soon wrinkles, faded blue eyes, wind-burned cheeks, pale yellow marks—maybe old bruises?—on her neck and hands.

"Coconut cream, too, please." She eyed the

waitress. Might have been the first time in a long time someone served her anything but a harsh word and the back of their hand.

"Thank you, um. . . " I looked at the waitress's name tag. "Carrie."

"So, I'm sorry, I didn't get your name. Are you from around here?" I felt really awkward, like I was out on a first date with an introvert and trying to get the conversation started.

"It's Toni with an 'i'. Heck, I didn't ask you your name, either." Toni stared at the table for a few minutes, fiddling with the salt and pepper shakers.

"Marla."

"Well, then, Marla, I was born in Oregon. A little town you probably never heard of. Brightwood. But I mostly tell folks I hail from Portland. It's easier than trying to explain." She smiled. "Where are you from?"

"Thanks, Carrie." I said to the waitress as two steaming mugs of coffee and two slices of pie were set on the table. Not really wanting to talk about myself, I picked up my mug, and inhaled the aroma deeply. "This coffee sure smells good! Me? I'm from Bangor, Maine."

"How long you been out here?" Toni picked up her coffee mug and sipped it delicately.

I was surprised at her good table manners. Somehow I'd expected her to gulp her food and belch. "Oh, about twenty years or so. I came here after college for a job, got married, had a family, and stayed." I took a forkful of pie and savored the delicious flavor for a moment. "How about you? What are you doing so far from home?"

"Well, my folks were crop pickers, and so we traveled a lot." She paused to eat. "Do you think we could get some more coffee?"

"Sounds like a hard life." I signaled to the waitress.

"It was, but it was a good life. Ma schooled us kids at home in the evenings as best she could, after work was done for the day. We moved around a lot, usually only staying in one place for a couple of weeks."

When the waitress appeared at our table, I smiled at her. She responded with a tiny life of one corner of her mouth. "Carrie, we'd like more coffee."

Carrie filled our cups again, and dropped some more creamers on the table.

I turned back to Toni. "Do you mind if I ask how you ended up on the streets?"

"Well, when I was about fourteen, my folks decided I needed some real schoolin'. They made arrangements with a family they picked for in Texas for me to live there with them. In exchange for my room and board, I would help out around the house and the farm." She took another bite of pie. "It worked out real good for about a year. Then the old man started making moves on me, and so I took off. I went to the last address I had for my family, but they had already moved on, and I had no way to start looking for them, so I was on my own."

She went on to tell about the next few years of struggling to find a place to live, hold down a job, and continue her education. It was hard, but she had a hunger to learn. She finished high school, and had even given community college a try, but ended up dropping out. That was three years ago. She had held a few jobs, but the hard economy meant that there were lots of people out there looking for the same few jobs. She had actually only been begging for a few weeks, since she was laid off from her last job as a building cleaner.

"I'm really just trying to get together enough money to travel on." She stared into her coffee a moment, then she smiled. "If I had any sense, I'd go south, like the birds."

I was amazed at how young this child looked when all the cares of the day were not etched on her thin face. *How much like my Kirsten she is.* "Want some more pie?"

"No, but thank you. I will have some more coffee, though."

"Me, too." I said, sitting back in my seat. This was the first time in months I'd actually felt myself relax. Somehow, life had gotten so complicated lately. And things at home had been falling apart for even longer. How good it would be to be as footloose as Toni was, going where you wanted, when. But that wasn't possible anymore.

The waitress hovered nearby, no doubt eavesdropping. She came right over when I signaled her and deftly filled our mugs to the brim. The aroma of freshly brewed coffee filled the place, and the smell of warm pie straight from the oven reminded me of growing up. How sad Toni didn't have those kind of memories.

"What would you do if you could do anything in the world?"

Toni interrupted my daydreams, and I jumped. Goodness, how far away had I been? "Well.... I haven't given it much thought, I guess." I replied carefully.

Even though Toni was nice to be around, still, you can't be too careful these days, can you? And anyway, that's a question I'd been afraid to ask myself. No point in dwelling on things that can never be.

"Come on. You must have wanted to do something when you were a kid that you haven't done yet." Toni persisted.

"Well, I always liked horses. I wanted to own a ranch, go riding whenever I wanted. I wanted a horse that would run, not like the worn out old nags we used to rent by the hour. I wanted—" I stopped, embarrassed at opening up like this. What was it about this child-woman that made me do that? I hadn't told anyone, not my husband, my kids, not even my best 'friend'.   Best friend, indeed.

I turned to look out the window, at nothing, really. I just didn't want Toni to see the tears that blurred my vision. My mother hadn't raised me to cry in public. Working very hard to get myself under control, I sipped my coffee, toyed with my fork, rearranged the napkin in my lap.

When I did finally look up, I was surprised to see tears in Toni's eyes, too.

She smiled shyly at me, as if we shared a great big secret. "I bet you never told anyone that, did you?"

I shook my head.

"Why didn't you ever do it?"

"Because I was too busy, we were too busy, the kids

were too busy, and now it's never going to happen because my husband is too busy with my best friend. I was on my way to file divorce papers when I met you." At this, I completely lost it, and broke down, right there at the table, where everyone in the coffee shop could see. Up until now, I'd managed to keep everything impersonal, cold, polite.

I'd never done this before. Why here? Why now? Why with this child?

Toni reached across the table, her hands weather-beaten and work-worn at such a young age and patted my carefully manicured hand. "It's never too late, you know."

"It's never too late for you to go back to school and get a real education." I countered, delicately wiping the end of my nose with the table napkin.

Toni paused a moment before answering. "And how did you know that was my dream?"

How to explain that I'd seen an excitement in her

face and hear a yearning in her voice as she told me about her missed opportunities at schoolin', as she called it. How her face had almost crumpled when she said she'd had to drop out of community college.

I sat there, astonished at the depth of my understanding for the young girl in such a short period of time. I knew here, because I *was* her. Oh, I had the education I thought I'd wanted. I had the husband—at least temporarily, the children, the house, the position, the friends.

But when I compared what I thought I wanted with my dreams, none of it measured up. For some reason, I had bared my soul, wanting to trust someone.

Several minutes went by as we stared at each other, not really seeing, but knowing. I wanted desperately to speak the thoughts that had been going around in my head and in my heart. *I want to take this child in, to nurture her, and teach her. Maybe we could both have our dreams together.* But something kept me from speaking the words.

Toni continued, "Last week I ran into a crop picker I used to know who told me my folks had settled in Wyoming. I've been talking with them, and they want me to come to live with them."

I nodded. She knew how I felt, about practically adopting her, and she was gently telling me that it wouldn't work. Everyone has plans, places to go, people who love them. And sticking around with me wasn't in her plans.

She sat back in her chair. "What you need to do is to go after your own dream, Marla. Buy some land. Find a job in a small town, so you can work near where you live. And get you some horses. Maybe a handsome ranch hand or two." Her eyes twinkled like stars in a night sky.

When had she gotten so wise?

"Oh Toni, I'm too old to be thinking about

romance."

"If I'm not too old to go back to school, why should you be too old for romance?" She stood. "I gotta go. I really want to get to Wyoming by the end of the week, and I still need about forty dollars for my bus fare. Gotta get back on the streets and look for money or work."

I dug in my purse for money for the bill and a generous tip. Then, because it was the only way I could think to help her, I pulled out two bills and pressed them into Toni's hand. "Say hi to your folks for me. Tell them if they don't treat you right they have to answer to me." I forced a smile I didn't yet feel.

Toni's eyes opened wide as she saw the money in her hand. "I will," she said. "And thanks, for everything." With that, she was gone, headed to the bus depot.

"You too." I called after her, although I'm pretty sure the door was closed by that time and she couldn't hear me.

Carrie gathered up the bill and the money. "Was everything all right?".

"Everything was perfect." This time my smile felt more genuine. Now I could see the possibility of a future that hadn't existed a few minutes before. Somehow, that child had shown me that it was time to stop living for others and to start making a life for myself. "That was the best cup of coffee I've had in years."

The Ticket

How could I have known that a simple day of shopping could turn so ugly?

In less than an hour, I was in and out of my local thrift store with the prizes I needed for the clubhouse Bingo Bonanza: boxed greeting cards. At home, I picked up the first box and leafed through the cards to make sure they weren't used. One year we didn't take the time, and a winner found a picture of a naked woman with lewd suggestions penned on the reverse of the picture, so we've checked them ever since.

At the bottom of the third box, a piece of color in the corner caught my eye. I couldn't hook it out with my fingernail, so I used a staple remover and peeled back the paper liner of the box. Pulling it out, I held it to the light, peering at the faded printing.

It was a pawn ticket. I felt bad that someone had tucked the ticket in this box. Funny how some people's lives ended up in second-hand stores.

There was nothing to identify the owner of the ticket, but the pawnshop name and information was there. Romantic scenes from old movies filled my imagination.

I picked up the phone and dialed the number on the ticket. While doing a good deed was, well, a good thing, no point wasting time and gas if the article had already been redeemed.

A gravelly voice answered the phone. "Chambers' Pawn. Raymond speaking."

"I have a ticket, and I want to know if the article is still there."

"That's the way it works. You bring in the ticket and

the money, and I give you the stuff."

"Can you tell me what the item is?"

"Nope. Bring it in."

"I found the ticket, and I wanted to return the item to the owner."

"Like I said, bring it in."

"Thanks. I'll think about it."

I hung up the phone and considered my options. I could just forget about it. Or I could play the Good Samaritan and go over there, buy the item, and try to convince the guy to tell me who brought it in. Or I could redeem the article and keep it or sell it.

I decided not to decide, just to go get it. I drove the couple of miles to a seedy part of town. Half of the storefronts were for sale or lease, and the other half were pawnshops or bars. Nice.

Chambers' Pawn Shop was in the middle of the

block, iron grills on the two front windows, and a sign warning that a dog patrolled the premises after hours. Real nice.

Raymond looked exactly as I'd pictured him from his gruff voice and gruffer attitude. He appeared to be eighty, but was probably more like sixty. Pasty skin from spending too much time indoors.

He looked up at me from a newspaper on the counter. "Yes?"

I set the ticket on the counter. "I'd like to redeem this."

He looked at the number, and I should have known something was up when he picked up the ticket and read the numbers aloud, one shoulder turned away from me, kind of facing a curtained opening behind the counter.

"Oh, yes, I remember you. You're the lady what called earlier." He peered at me over his half-glasses then set the ticket on the counter. "I'll be right back."

He disappeared behind the curtain, and hushed voices filtered past the overhead fan. I couldn't catch much, but one phrase didn't make sense at the time: no trouble in here.

I waited until the old man reappeared, holding a small wooden box with brass and ivory inlays.

He set it on the counter next to my ticket and ran a hand over the surface. "Nice little box. Guy said it belonged to his mother. Sentimental value." He smiled, a gold crown glinting from his left canine. "Course, he said he was coming back for it." He shook his head. "Can't trust people."

I opened the box. It was empty. Just like my understanding of why anyone would pawn this. "How much?"

"Ten bucks plus the interest for the month. Twenty

should do it."

I fished the bill from my purse and handed it over. "I was expecting maybe a diamond necklace or a suitcase full of money."

He didn't join in my laughter, although I thought it was pretty funny.

He pushed a ledger book toward me. Using his index finger, he pointed to a line. "Sign here."

I followed his directions while trying to read the hen scratch writing that gave the name and address of the owner of the ticket. Marty Rivers? Mark Rogers? Mary Roggins?

He snatched the book from my grasp. "Private information."

"I wanted to return the box to the owner."

"Won't do you no good. He died. About ten days ago."

I shivered as if a goose had walked over my grave, took the box, and left the shop. When I got to my car, I tossed the box on the seat then locked the car doors, mostly out of habit, but also because of mistrust for the neighborhood. Call me chicken.

The box bounced then rolled off, hitting the floor with a thud. I reached over and picked it up. One of the ends of the box felt loose.

"Great, I paid twenty bucks for it and now it's falling apart."

I tried to press the piece back in, but it wouldn't go. It was like there was something wedged in there, keeping it from slipping into place.

Using my car key, I pried at the end until it popped off in my hand. I tossed that piece on the seat and went back to the box. Pressing on the inside part, I felt something underneath the veneer. Using my key again as a tool, I peeled off the veneer lining, and a key dropped into my lap.

Just what I needed, yet another mystery.

A loud bang on my driver's side window startled me, and I dropped the key in my lap. Looking up, a man's face, ugly in its anger, stared back at me. He worked the door latch, trying to open the door.

On the passenger side, another man pounded on the window with a closed fist and screamed at me. Ignoring their request, I jammed my car key in the ignition, started the engine, and blasted out of there. In my rearview mirror, Dumb shook his fist at me as Dumber ran to a nearby convertible, jumped in the front seat, and gunned the motor.

I took the first right then a left in front of a bus. The driver screeched the brakes and blasted on the horn. A couple more turns, then I doubled back on Broadway in the curb lane, a large panel van obscuring me from the traffic in the oncoming lane. Sure enough, Dumb and Dumber went past in the opposite direction, oblivious to the fact I was going the other way.

I wasn't sure it would be safe to go home right now, so I went to the nearest library. Logging on to the computer, I did an internet search for the variations of the names I'd seen in the ledger book, eliminating Mary because the pawnshop guy said "he". I struck it big. A couple weeks before, Mark Rogers and two accomplices robbed a local bank of somewhere in the neighborhood of two hundred and fifty thousand dollars. Mark's body was found in a rundown rooming house three days later. He'd been beaten to death and his room searched thoroughly. His two buddies were still on the loose.

The only thing I could figure was Mark hid the money then tried to hold out on his friends. They didn't like that arrangement and worked him over. Mark's double-cross included hiding the money and then the key. Pawning the box kept it safe from their prying eyes. And, as he'd told Raymond, he had every intention of retrieving the box, probably when his friends were apprehended. Maybe they saw him pawn the box, but didn't realize its importance at the time, and if they didn't know about the trick end piece, they'd never have found the key.

The key wasn't for a safety deposit box. The airport and bus station were out, since they stopped using lockers years ago. A public storage locker maybe, but that seemed like overkill for what was probably a couple of duffle bags of money at the most.

Although I'd never robbed a bank or been on the lam from the cops, I tried to put myself in this guy's head. Where would I hide that much money?

As I browsed through the various businesses that

offered storage, I came across a listing for a company that sold safes for hotels. That gave me an idea.

Maybe Mark bought a safe. Where would he hide it? From the sounds of the article in the paper, his accomplices worked Mark and his place over pretty well and didn't find a safe.

Maybe he rented a safe? How would a person go about doing that?

A hotel safe. Lots of hotel rooms had safes or provided them for their guests. Now I needed to find the hotel room.

I logged off the computer and went back to the parking lot. Dumb and Dumber leaned against the hood of my car. I ducked back into the library. There had to be another exit.

In the children's area of the library, a door led to a fenced area. As casually as my racing heart and shaking knees would allow, I walked through the doorway and followed the fence line to the gate. Bushes separated the parking lot from the play area, and I ducked down below the height of the shrubs. At the next cross street, a bus pulled up to the stop. I jogged to the bus and hopped aboard, dropping some change in the fare box.

I watched out the window as the bus rolled past the parking lot. The two goons were still leaning against my car. Dumber pointed at the library, Dumb pointed at the car, and Dumber pointed an index finger into Dumb's chest. Looked like their friendship was going south.

Just as I was. South away from the library. Apart from that, I had no idea what I was looking for until I saw a locksmith's shop. I pulled the cord to signal I wanted off then turned to my right and fast-walked back to the shop.

A man at a key cutting machine polished a key for the customer ahead of me.

When my turn came, I passed the key to the locksmith. "I need a copy."

He peered through a monocle at the key then shook his head. "Can't do it. Code says this can't be copied." He pushed the key back to me. "This is for a hotel safe."

"If I lost it, could someone tell what hotel it's for?"

"If they had the code book."

"Would you show me how that works?"

He raised one eyebrow then shrugged and pulled a dog-eared notebook from under the counter. Licking an index finger, he thumbed through the booklet until he found the code. "Somerset Hotel over on Maynard and Waters."

I nodded. "I'll get a copy of this other key, if you don't mind." I gave him my house key. I didn't really need another copy but thought I should buy something to thank him for his help.

Five minutes later, I was out of there and on my way to the Somerset. Except I didn't have my car. It was back at the library. Rats.

I flagged down a cab and resigned myself to the twenty-dollar cab ride. Oh well, with all that bank money waiting for me at the hotel, I could afford it. Even if I never saw a dime of the bank money, I'd had more excitement today than in the past ten years combined. It was worth every penny.

I've got to start being more careful about what I say. No sooner were the words thought than we turned the corner on Maynard. Cops filled the sidewalk, the SWAT van filled the four spaces directly in front of the Somerset, and K-9 dogs sniffed the crowd.

I got the driver to stop a couple of doors before the hotel, paid my fare, and got out. A cluster of people watched from behind a police line, so I mingled with them, hoping to overhear what was going on. One guy with a name tag reading "Somerset Hotel, Walter, Front Desk Clerk" commented maybe it had to do with the unclaimed hotel safe someone found in an empty room.

My ears perked up at that pronouncement. I nudged Walter with my elbow. "What's that about an unclaimed safe?"

He turned to face me. "Who are you?"

I put on my best smile. "Jones from the Tribune covering the excitement. And your name is?"

He puffed his chest and pulled back his shoulders a tad. "Walter. I'm the front desk clerk here. Housekeeping found the safe. The guy who rented the room paid for two weeks. We haven't seen him for about ten days, and since he was supposed to check out today, we went in to clean the room. Well, the safe was there, and it was locked, and the guest had the only key, so we called the police to report it, in case he came back to claim it. They checked him out, found out the name he gave us was bogus. Imagine that."

I nodded, eager for him to continue.

"They sent an officer to investigate, who collected some fingerprints and had them identified." Raymond leaned in closer to me, the garlic from his lunch assaulting my nose. "Seems the guy was murdered right after he rented the room. So the police hope the money is in the safe."

I feigned innocence. "Money?" *Surely not* my *money. Please God, not my money.*

"The money he and two other guys stole from a bank." Raymond stood back and crossed his arms over his chest, his story told.

My money. Gone, just like that. Before I even had a chance to struggle over whether I should turn it in or not.

Just as well, I guess.

That might be a struggle I would lose.

Especially if Dumb and Dumber ever found me.

So, like I said, I'd gotten my money's worth of excitement.

One thing I learned from all of this: the next time I go to the second-hand store to buy prizes for Bingo Bonanza, I'm checking the box before I buy it. And if there's a ticket inside, I'm putting it back on the shelf.

Poppy's Story
(Originally published in The Liguorian, February 2004)

"As I recall, the story goes something like this..." That was the way he always began his stories, my grandfather. We sat on the edge of our seats, so to speak, to hear the next part of the story. Always there was that long, pregnant pause. Then he would clear his throat with a loud "Hrrrmmmph!" that made us jump.

"Just checking to make sure you're paying attention" he would say with a chuckle. My grandpa, as if we could fall asleep!

"It all began when I was a young man. My family was living in New Haven, in a rickety little house on the beach. That's all we could afford in those days. Living was tough, and my dad was gone all the time." He paused to take another puff on his pipe. How we loved that old pipe. Tobacco smoke wafting around the room. To this day when I smell chocolate pipe tobacco I can see him in his old chair, puffing contentedly away.

"Yep, my dad was gone all the time, either fishin', or in the woods, cutting wood for the local mill. Those were hard times, let me tell you. And since I was the only boy, it was left to me to help my mother run the house." Gnarled fingers held over the bowl of the pipe kept it burning just right -- not too fast, but not too slow that there was too much effort in the smoke.

"Ayah, this partic'lar event happened the winter before I left home to go to college in the city. Course, at the time, I didn't know I'd be going to college. No one in our family ever had. Why, most never even got through school before they had to go working in the woods, or on the boats. That's not to say we weren't smart," he added, just to make sure we didn't think that. "We just never had any money for schooling and such. But my dad always wanted something more for his kids than what he'd had. Dad was in the woods, and that had been a real hard winter. Lots of ice and snow. Even the game was scarce, and we'd seen a wolf or two around the town, snooping for food. It was February. I 'member that, 'cuz everyone was saying 'A hard February means a full graveyard'. Guess I didn't really know what they meant until that year." He paused again, and looked around at the group of us.

"I think you're all falling asleep. Let's finish this tomorrow night." he said, with a twinkle in his eye, making a move to get out of his chair.

Of course we all protested as much and as loudly as we could. "No, Poppy, finish it now! We aren't tired. Really we aren't." And if one of our number had fallen asleep, we poked them until they woke up, just to prove our interest in the outcome of the story.

"Well, all right, I'll go on another bit, then. Settle down, now, and listen." Pause, puff on the pipe, ease back into the chair. Scratch the dog's head a minute or so while we settled into the cushions again.

"Like I said, it was February. A colder, darker night I've never seen. And my mother said she had run out of wood for the stove. Now, in those days, the wood stove was all that kept us from freezing to death. Not like houses these days, with their central heating. I mean, it was sometimes so cold when you got up in the morning that the pottie was frozen over. And
going to the outhouse, well that was a trip you saved for special occasions, let me tell you." He let out a mighty laugh at the thought of that, loud enough to wake up the younger ones who had fallen asleep again. He patiently waited until we all settled back again, basking in the

warmth from the fire.

"Being the oldest, I was the one to go for the wood. We didn't have a lot of lights back then, either. All we had was the one oil lamp in the house, so I had to go out in the pitch black. Course I knew my way around the back garden like the back of my hand. But you know yourself how different things look at night." He looked around the group for confirmation of our understanding of what he was saying. And while none of us had ever been out in the dark of night without a light, we all nodded. We could almost see how dark it was, just from his telling it.

"So there I was, kind of stumbling about on the snow and ice, trying to remember where the woodshed was, trying to pick it out of the dozen other dark shapes looming over me in the yard. And all the while, I was sure wolves or a bear, was following me, sniffing my tracks." With this, he leaned forward, his gnarled old fingers held in the shape of claws. The light from the fire cast eery shadows on the wall opposite. One of the younger kids, who had chosen this moment to wake up, saw the giant claws on the wall. He jumped up, screamed, and ran from the room, calling for his mother.

"Dad, are you scaring those kids again? They'll never sleep tonight if you keep that up." my mother called from the next room. We could hear her trying to soothe the small child, all the while tsk-tsking at Poppy for scaring a small child half to death.

But that was what we were here for! We wanted to be scared, at least a little.

"Anyway," he continued, ignoring my mother, just like always. "Just before I got to the woodshed, I heard this low growl behind me. I stopped dead in my tracks, turned slowly, and saw two pairs of yellow eyes staring at me. Wolves! I thought I was done for. And I couldn't tell which way to run. Wolves behind me, the ocean roaring off to one side, the dark woods to the other side, and somewhere in between, the wood shed. Just then, I heard it."

Maddeningly, he stopped again, and took several puffs on his pipe, watching the smoke swirl over our heads to the ceiling.

"Heard what?" I demanded, not wanting him to stop, even to breathe. "You can't stop now, Poppy!"

"I heard a voice call out to me. It was my father's voice. But it couldn't have been, 'cuz, like I said, he was away in the woods, a hundred miles north. And he warn't due back for three more weeks. At first I thought maybe he got in early, but then...." his voice trailed off.

"Then what, Poppy? Don't stop now, just when it's getting good." we protested.

"Then I saw that he warn't really there, and it warn't really him. I mean, it kinda sounded like my dad, 'cuz I could hear his voice, and sorta see him, but I could see through him at the same time. Now you know I don't abide with foolishness like ghosts and such, and I didn't as a young man, either. But I know what I saw, and I know I saw my Dad there that night."

"W-w-what did he say to you, Poppy?" asked one of the younger ones, trembling with fear, wide-eyed at the thought of what might be coming.

"At first he just sorta stood there, glowin' in the dark. He kinda lit up the whole yard. I could see where everything was just like in the daylight. The wolves saw him, too. And they just turned tail and ran. Then I realized it warn't my dad. This thing said 'Howard, your dad has done all he can for you. You need to look after your mom and the girls.' And then he just sorta melted away, is the only way I can describe it."

With that, he paused again. This time, instead of

puffing on his pipe, he pulled out an old wrinkled handkerchief, and blew noisily into it.

"Well, I realized it was some kind of Angel of God, with a message for me, and me alone. About two days later we got word that my dad had taken a bad fall off a tree he was chopping, and had died before they could get help to him. And that had happened at the very time I saw that angel in the garden. But more amazing than his appearing to me like that was the fact he had been there when I needed him the most. If he hadn't shown up when he did, I believe I'd have been eaten by those wolves. I don't know for sure just how God knew I was in trouble at that very moment. Except that He always knows when His children need Him, just like any good parent would. Just like my dad did. What I can say is that ever since then, I've never really felt alone. I know He is still looking out for me.

"But that isn't the end of the story. It's really just the beginning. My dad had bought life insurance on hisself, and that money helped to pay for my university education. So you see, it was an ending, but it was also a beginning. A beginning of an education that I sorely wanted. A beginning of a way out of a life of poverty for me and my family. And the beginning of a relationship with God that gets better and better each day. And that's the best kind of a story, don't you think?"

One Hot Summer's Night

Sitting there in the crowded tent, fanning her face to keep the mosquitoes away, she wondered for the umpteenth time what in the world had she been thinking, coming here tonight, of all nights? This circus had been in town all week, and she had purposely avoided coming. Her friends had used all forms of manipulation to get her to join them, but she had managed to resist them. And then tonight, of all nights, she had evaded them once more, only to change her mind at the last minute, and come here, alone.

Alone? How could you be alone in a tent filled with hundreds of profusely sweating bodies? Everywhere she looked, faces glistened and eyes shone with perspiration. Of course, here in the south, women didn't sweat, they 'dew'. Laura looked around for a familiar face, then remembered that she wasn't supposed to be here at all. After that, she carefully avoided making any eye contact with anyone.

And what was she really here for? If this was really all a joke, was her presence required to prove it? Because, really, it had to be a joke, right? They couldn't possibly do the things they claimed they could do. Because if they could, there would be more people here than there were, right? Word would have gotten out, people would be flocking here by the droves, wanting some of what they had.

Unless no one else believed they could do it, just like she didn't believe. Her friends claimed that what they said was true, but was there really any proof? No. She had to come to see for herself.

The crowd hushed as a man came onto the small stage in the front of the tent. Everyone seemed to be holding their breath, not wanting to miss a single word. Laura was waiting, too, to see what all the excitement was about. After all, it wasn't like she didn't need some of what they were giving away. She leaned slightly forward and to the left so that she could see around the taller person sitting in front of her. Why do people wear big hats and sit up front, blocking the view of everyone behind them?

Actually, Laura's initial reaction was disappointment as she watched the man on the stage. He man looked so ordinary, that had she passed him on the street, she would not have noticed him at all. He stood for a moment, eyes closed, motionless, face raised slightly to the sky. Then his voice filled the tent, and echoed off the hills outside. Without benefit of any form of amplification, Laura was startled when the words were so loud that they were *inside her soul* She looked around at the people near her. Each one was hypnotized by his words; even the children had stopped fidgeting and were listening attentively.

So this is how he does it, she thought. *He has us under a magic spell, and we don't know it. Just like those sorcerers who come with their useless magic potions.* With that, she decided to leave this charlatan and his groupies.

As she struggled to get to her feet, however, she glanced at the speaker one more time. His eyes bored into her very being, and she was frozen in place. All around her, the people sat, transfixed by him. Excerpt now he wasn't talking to them, he was talking to her, and to her alone. He told her all about her life, about the things she had done. She looked around in embarrassment, mortified to have these secret sins revealed to this crowd. But by the looks on their faces, she could tell they hadn't heard a word he had said. Were these words for her, and for her alone?

    Her legs shook, unable to bear her weight any longer. Her hands were damp with the exertion of standing up, and, unable to keep her grip, her crutches fell to the floor. She jumped at the sharp noise, and then realized that she was standing by herself, for the first time in her life. The speaker was beckoning her to come to him. His arms were stretched towards her, his palms turned upwards. Tentatively, she took a small step, still unsure of what was happening to her. He smiled, encouraging her in her newfound mobility. She took another step, and another, and then was running down the center aisle towards the front where he stood, still smiling at her.

Running. Something she'd never been able to do before. Born with crooked legs and a hunched back, she had endured stares and taunts all her life. She had gotten used to avoiding making eye contact. It was too painful to see someone staring at her, and, when caught in their staring, for them to not look at her again. Even her own family had treated her like she wasn't there, talking about her, around her, for her, but rarely to her.

Running. One foot in front of the other, in quick succession. Faster than a walk, faster even than a trot. She ran, feeling her hair flying behind her, even if for just a few moments. How she had wanted to run as a child, to join her friends in their play. But always, she had been kept inside, hidden, somehow her deformity an embarrassment to her family.

Especially her mother. She knew how much her mother suffered. How many days had she wished Laura had not been born? How many times had she blamed God for the imperfect limbs? The back that would never stand tall and straight? How many times had Laura herself done the same thing?

As she drew near to him, she looked up at him once again. She forgot who she was as she gazed into the depths of his eyes. He knew everything about her, and he didn't avert his eyes. Suddenly, Laura knew that what they had said was true. If she couldn't believe the miracle of her healing, she could believe her eyes.

The palms of his hands were scarred.

The Kid-a-pult

I sat on the park bench that humid August morning. When I'd arrived about an hour before, the grass bore a fresh coat of dew, the redwing blackbirds sang in the linden tree that shaded where I sat, and the sun was but a sliver on the horizon.

I love early mornings. Each new day seems to carry the opportunity for something exciting and unexpected to happen. This particular morning, a small rabble of swallowtail butterflies lit in the tree beside me, turning the previously-green foliage into a mesmerizing collage of yellows and browns.

I like to think of myself as alone but not lonely. If you asked my neighbors, they might describe me as a crotchety old man who needs to get out more. I've heard them talking over their fences.

Or they might say I need a wife to look after me.

Huh! I enjoy my bachelor status. When my Emma was here, we enjoyed our married state to the fullest. The only sorrow in our lives was that we never had children. Maybe if we had, folks wouldn't be in such a hurry to marry me off again. As it was, Emma's leave-taking was still as fresh in my mind as if it were yesterday instead of a year ago.

In some ways, today was an anniversary. Three hundred and sixty-five days ago, Emma flew off to heaven, leaving me behind to miss her every day. Yes, maybe having children would have made a difference.

A squeal called me back from my musings to the present. On the swing set just across the grassy expanse, two children clambered onto a seat each. The older one, a girl of about six, leaned way back, her hands gripping the chains, then leaned forward, pulling her legs beneath the swing, chattering to the little fellow beside her.

"See, Matthew, this is how you get the swing going when there's no grown-ups to help." She repeated the process several times, gaining a couple of inches with each effort, until she swung to and fro.

The boy, Matthew, sat unmoving and apparently unconvinced.

"Come on, Matthew, try."

"Don't know how to, Emma."

My heart skipped a beat at the sound of the little girl's name. Same as my Emma. And the little fellow's name, while not exactly like mine, at Matthew was close enough to Matthias to catch my attention. And my heart.

I pushed myself to my feet and walked over to the two. Emma continued swinging, dependent on nobody for her enjoyment. Matthew turned to look at me as I stood behind him.

I nodded at him. "Want me to push you?"

A smile covered his face and he nodded. "Yes, sir. Thank you, sir."

I grabbed the edge of the swing seat and pulled it toward me. With a mighty heave, strength in me I didn't even know I still had, I pushed him forward. Up he went, legs stretched forward, body leaning back. On the return swing, I pushed him again, and higher he went. This time, as he leaned back, he closed his eyes, enjoying the ride.

As he swung higher, Emma, surprised by his sudden progress, leaned back on the upswing, exertion evident in her flushed face. She laughed, a wonderful giggle starting in her tummy and working its way up until she released it to dance on the morning breeze. "No fair, Matthew. You've got help."

Matthew challenged her. "Didn't say I couldn't get help. This man is my angel, Emma."

On Emma's return swing, as she leaned her head way back, she studied me, her large blue eyes wide with wonder. I bowed and tipped my head to her.

"Are you a real angel, mister?" She hadn't been convinced by her brother.

"I am if Matthew says I am." I gave her swing a push to even things out.

She squealed in joy, and then our adventure became a contest between the two to see who could swing the highest. At one point, the chains holding the swings caught some slack at the height of their extension because of how high the children went.

And I was transported back to just one year ago today, the day Emma left. We had both climbed on the swings, foolishness, I know, for eighty-year-olds. But that day, we felt like we were eight. And we leaned and pumped, challenging each other to reach greater heights, to snap the chains, to risk it all for the sake of the contest.

And then Emma won. She soared off the swing, high into the sky, as if she'd been caught on a fantastic fishing line from heaven, propelled by the faith that had united and strengthened us all our lives. I watched her rise, a smile on her face as she waved good-bye to me. An ache filled my heart because I'd been afraid to push that one bit harder, to rise that one inch higher.

I continued to push the children, alternating between one and the other. But I didn't push them high enough to realize the potential of the kid-a-pult. No siree, I was reserving that for myself, later, after they'd gone.

I just knew if I tried hard enough, I'd be able to join Emma and share in that certain knowledge that all of God's promises were true.

Sanctuary Here

The walk to her best friend Mona's house always invigorated Brenda, which was why she offered to do the walking and let Mona do the hostessing. Mona answered the door and laughed at the sight of her bundled up in her winter parka, a scarf wrapped around her face, and her hands shoved deep into her pockets.

"Come in. No point heating the entire neighborhood."

Brenda pushed past Mona into the foyer of the century-old house. "Ooo-eee, it sure is cold out there. Brrrrr! What a great morning to be getting together!"

"I'm glad I don't have to go out in that cold this morning, that's for sure." Mona reached to take Brenda's coat and hung the garment on the coat rack in the hallway. "I don't know how much longer we'll be getting together here, though."

"What?" Brenda wasn't sure she had heard

correctly. "What do you mean, not get together? We've been having coffee here for what seems like a hundred years. Why, Tuesday mornings just wouldn't be the same, somehow. Take that back, Mona."

She mock-slapped her friend's arm, certain she was being teased. Mona liked to play practical jokes but this was taking it a bit too far. Kind of like joking that God wouldn't always be there.

"Come, let's sit in the kitchen, where it's nice and warm. What was I thinking, springing that on you like that?"

Brenda followed her friend down the long hallway that ran through the length of the old house. Several rooms opened off the hallway on either side—living room, two bedrooms, a bathroom, and in the back, the large family-size kitchen.

Knowing Mona as well as she did, Brenda knew the story behind this house. Mona's family had owned the house in Bayview for as long as either of them could remember. Mona had grown up in the house, along with her older sister, Margaret. Her parents had died more than twenty years before, and, although the house had been left to Margaret, Mona and her husband, Carl, continued to live there, using the furniture, contents, and a small legacy left to her.

For years, Margaret, who was married and lived outside Boston, had told anyone who would listen that she didn't want to come back to live in the small town of Bayview. It was too far to commute to her important job in banking and her husband's important work at the shipyards. Besides, it wasn't even in a particularly fashionable part of Massachusetts.

So Mona and Carl lived there, enjoying the small town atmosphere. Mona said it was the best place to raise a family. Carl, who was originally from the West Coast, liked to be near the ocean, and so he was satisfied near just about any ocean. They'd raised their daughter Chloe here, had seen her married in their backyard, and were now awaiting the birth of their first grandchild.

Their life seemed so perfect.

Until today.

Mona busied herself laying out biscuits and cookies on her mother's china plates. "Do you want coffee? I have some of that flavored creamer that you like, the Irish Crème one." She filled Brenda's cup from the silver coffee service her mother received as an anniversary gift along with the matching he tray, sugar bowl, and creamer. "And take a cookie. No, two."

"Yes, that's fine. Now tell me, what is going on?"

Mona stood beside the table, her hands shaking so badly Brenda was certain she would drop the pot.

She laid a hand on her friend's arm. "For goodness sake, set that down before you break something."

Mona sank into her chair. She buried her face in her hands and sobbed. "I don't know what we're going to do. We're going to have to leave here."

Brenda knew better than to interrupt her friend right now. Sometimes the best thing you can do for a friend, especially one you've known for over forty years, is to let them cry themselves out. So Brenda filled in her time by adding creamer to her cup and leaving Mona's cup black, just as she liked it. Then she went to the bathroom and brought back the box of tissues, placing it on the table within reach.

She sipped her coffee, feeling the liquid warm her from the inside out. As she waited for Mona's tears to subside, she looked around the familiar kitchen.

Mona was a consummate housekeeper, having been a homemaker ever since she married Carl nearly twenty-five years before. He insisted he would support his family, and Mona had often told Brenda how she enjoyed being able to devote her time and energies to keeping house.

She and Mona had been friends since grade school and had gone through a lot together. Carl had once joked he was glad she and his wife were friends, since it gave Mona someone else to worry over, leaving her less time to worry over him. In many ways, Brenda envied her friend, although she knew Mona thought Brenda lived the glamorous life.

As a professional photographer, Brenda had worked

for several of the major fashion magazines over the years. Many of her photos made the cover of these magazines, and the top models asked for her by name. She had traveled the world several times over, spending little time at home in Bayview. However, she liked the small-town laid-back atmosphere because it was such a contrast to her work life. Even though there were some years when she spent less than a month there in total, she decided to keep her small cottage near the beach.

Her lifestyle was not conducive to marriage, and Brenda had never found a man who was willing to live in her shadow. Or one she was willing to give up her career for. Sure, she'd had her share of relationships, and even an engagement. But most men were put off by the hectic pace of her job.

The only things that endured were Mona and this house. Whenever Brenda was in Bayview, Tuesday mornings were spent with Mona. In fact, Brenda had spent more time in this house with Mona than most people even knew. Many times when she was in Boston, she drove down to get away from the hustle and bustle of the city.

Then there had been the sudden end to that disastrous affair in Paris, and she had flown home in the middle of the big Vogue shoot to cry on Mona's shoulder, in the living room, looking out on the main street.

There had been the mammogram scare, when Mona held her in the hallway where she had collapsed from fear and exhaustion, assuring her that everything was going to be all right.

And it was. Mona was rarely wrong, somehow.

She had come right away when Mona's mother had taken ill suddenly, sitting there with her friend when her mother died three days later. This was her time to hold her friend and remind her that it was going to be okay.

And again when Mona's father, unable and unwilling to live without his soul mate, passed away less than three months later, they cried, sitting here at this very table.

She hadn't been able to attend Chloe's wedding, but had come just before to help with the planning and bridal shower.

This house. It was such a big part of their relationship. And the things in the house—the china plates they used every time they got together that had belonged to Mona's mother. The only other time she used the service was for company and holidays.

When Brenda had asked her about that, Mona had stood, hands on hips, and stared at her as if she had three heads. Then she'd said, "First of all, it isn't every day I get to entertain a famous photographer, so that makes it special."

Brenda had laughed. "What's the second thing?"

"Having my best friend with me is a holiday of sorts, so that makes it extra special."

Every room held such special memories for her, but the kitchen was her favorite. Even though it was big, big enough to have the dining table and still leave room for eight chairs and a china cabinet, the room felt intimate. Mona had painted the walls and ceiling a robin's egg blue, and then stenciled a wonderful collage of wildflowers as a border. The delightful yellows, purples, and golds started at the doorway to the kitchen and wound up the wall, around the ceiling, down around the cabinets and window, and out to the back door leading to the mud room. She had even stenciled a smaller version on the kitchen cabinets, around the light switch and outlets, and around the base of the light fixture in the ceiling.

Everywhere you looked, you felt like you were in the middle of a huge field of life and beauty.

Brenda felt safe in this house. Safer than anywhere else in the world. The doors were never locked, creating a sense of old-world security. Bayview was still small enough there was no need. *The day might come soon enough for that*, Brenda mused to herself. *It's nice there is still somewhere in this world where locks aren't needed.*

The house always smelled like home. Mona made her own bread, baked cookies several times a week, and made sure Carl had a hearty home-cooked meal on the table every night at six. You could set your watch by that. Brenda had eaten many fine meals here, and once joked that Mona was a one-woman weight gain clinic.

Brenda shook herself back to the present. Whatever was going on must be stopped. She couldn't lose this house. She couldn't lose *them*.

Mona had almost stopped crying by this point, and was noisily blowing her nose, tossing embarrassed glances at her friend from behind her tissues. "I'm sorry to make a fool of myself." She wiped her eyes. "I just didn't know how to tell you, and—"

"It's okay to cry with a friend once in a while, you know. How many times have I cried with you? It must be payback time." Brenda tried to sound a lot perkier than she felt. Actually, she felt like Mona looked—like her heart had been ripped out. "Now, start at the beginning, and tell me what is going on."

Mona took a deep breath then paused to sip her coffee. "I make good coffee, don't I?"

Brenda nodded, hesitant to interrupt, lest it cause Mona to start crying again.

"The beginning. Well, let's see." Mona stopped, as

if searching for the words. Her eyes welled up with tears again. "Margaret is retiring and thinks I've lived here in this house long enough, and wants to move back to Bayview to live, and she wants to live here, and so we're going to have to move!" She drew a breath and collapsed in tears again.

"Margaret, moving back to Bayview to live? Why, she said when she was here for Chloe's wedding that Bayview was the dullest place on earth. According to her, it's like living on the dark side of the moon. She said she'd rather live in Borneo than live here. Why does she think she has any right to kick you out of your house?"

Mona gathered herself together again. "It's not my house. The house was left to her. I got the furniture and some money. Margaret didn't want to sell it, and she didn't want us to have to pay a mortgage to buy her out, so we agreed to live here, keep it up, pay the taxes. Carl and I spent a lot of money on it over the years, digging out the basement, replacing the roof, upgrading the bathroom and kitchen. We always just thought of it as being our house."

"Can't you just tell her no? You've got squatters rights, don't you?"

Mona shook her head. "We never dreamed Margaret would waltz back into town and expect to take it back." Mona stood to refill the coffee pot from the urn on the counter. "She hasn't even been here since Chloe got married, and that was four years ago. And that was the first time since our parents died."

"Did you have a legal agreement drawn up when you first moved in? You know, spelling out what each person's rights were?"

"Legal agreement? We may not be close, but she is my sister!" Mona returned to the table. "We never thought a legal agreement would be needed."

Brenda held up one hand. "Just asking. Might have come in handy just about now, though."

"You're right, and I'm sorry. This has me so upset. Where will we go? What will we do with all of our things?" Mona looked like she was getting ready to cry again. Red blotches crept up her neck, and her eyes watered.

"Do you have any money saved? Could you buy the house and let her buy something else?"

"We should have done that twenty years ago, when house prices were more reasonable. But now, even here in Bayview, the market has risen so much. And Carl was looking forward to retiring in the next couple of years. He wouldn't do that if we had a mortgage." Mona dabbed at her nose. "What will Tuesdays be like if we aren't in this house? It's much more than a house to Carl and me. It's a sanctuary."

Brenda contemplated her friend's words. Yes, sanctuary was the perfect description. A place where life had to stay outside the door and not enter unless invited. Safe and protected from the world, evil barricaded out, a friend who was closer than family to confide in. What would Tuesdays, or Thursdays, or any day, for that matter, be like if they weren't in this house?

Then Brenda realized the answer was right in front of her. Sitting in front of her, actually.

"Mona, Mona!" She clapped her hands. "Don't you see? It isn't this house. This house is not important. What's important is us. You. Me. Us. Tuesdays will still be Tuesdays, no matter where in the world we are, because of us. You can't even begin to count the number of Tuesdays when I wasn't here that I would look at my watch and say 'Oh, it's ten o'clock in Bayview. I wonder what Mona's doing'. Don't you see? This house isn't our sanctuary. We are our sanctuary. The laughs, the tears, the long talks, the long silences. That's our sanctuary, and that can be anywhere we are."

Mona chewed on her bottom lip a while, then her eyes lit up. She stopped sniffling. Then she cocked her head to one side. "We can have Tuesdays anywhere. And Thursdays. Any day we need it to be."

"You've got it, my friend!" Brenda nodded. "And I know right where I want it to be, from now on. My cottage sits empty most of the time. Why don't you and Carl move in? Take all your things you need and leave the rest here for Margaret."

The smile dropped from her friend's face. "But you won't have a place to live."

"Sure I will. I'm only home for a few days at a time anyway. The cottage has two bedrooms, and we can stand each other's company for that long, can't we?"

"You're right. Oh, it sounds too good to be true." Mona paused. "I'll have to make sure Carl is fine with this before we get too far into the planning."

"I'm sure he'll agree. You know he loves me like a sister. And do you know the best part?"

"What's that?"

"Now I won't have to go out in the cold to join you for coffee!"

The Prodigal Returns

Meg was in the midst of making a pie, ingredients strewn all over the kitchen, when she heard a noise at the door. Expecting it to be her husband John, she waited for his customary hug-from-behind. When a moment or two passed, and his arms were still not around her, she turned slowly, intending to tease him for forgetting her hug.

In the middle of her turn, a soft voice spoke. "Are you so mad at me that you won't even say 'hi'?"

"Bethy, Bethy! Is that really you?" Meg couldn't believe her eyes. "Oh, how I've missed you, sister!" Ever since Beth had left town, Meg hadn't heard from her. When their parents died within months of each other, she'd posted the notices in the local papers, hoping against hope that Beth was still in the area. Still no word.

"I missed you, too, Meggy."

"Where have you been all this time?"

"How about some coffee, and then we can talk?"

"Oh, I'm not being much of a hostess, am I?" Meg turned to the coffee maker, but her hands shook so badly she couldn't pour the coffee. "I don't know why I'm so clumsy."

Beth came up behind her and touched her shoulder. Her voice, when she spoke, was soft, timid almost. "Meggy, I didn't mean to upset you."

"You aren't upsetting me. Well, I was a mite peeved when you left town like that…" She crossed her arms over her chest, inviting an explanation. "So what happened?"

"I wondered how long before you got to that."

Meg was half afraid to ask the next question. "Are you home for good?"

"I'm home. God brought me here, for this time, and I'll stay, if you'll have me."

"Have you? Sit, tell me everything that's happened since I saw you last."

They settled at the kitchen table, a cup of coffee in front of each, and took turns filling in the gap that time had created in their lives. The years slipped away as they began at the beginning—when Beth left town.

When they finally got caught up, Meg looked at the clock over the sink. "My goodness, it's nearly supper time, and I haven't got my pie done or supper started. John will be home soon, and he'll be hungry. Funny he never showed up for lunch. He always calls if he isn't coming home."

"Maybe he got busy."

"Hmm. I'll call and see what's up. Then you can tell me why God brought you home."

Meg turned to the phone and lifted the receiver to dial. But seeing a strange car pull up in her driveway, she hung the phone up. A man in a dark suit got out of the car and slowly walked up the driveway.

She pulled back the lace curtain. "I wonder who that is?"

Beth joined her at the window as the stranger rang the bell. The tones of the doorbell jolted Meg out of her reverie. She went to answer the door, a knot of foreboding like a piece of unchewed meat stuck in her throat.

"Mrs. Blackstone?" His cultured voice bespoke years of education. Or perhaps simply a good upbringing. "Are you Mrs. Blackstone?"

"Yes, I'm Meg Blackstone."

"Mrs. Blackstone, I'm Detective Carl Bohn from the Highway Patrol. May I come in for a moment?"

"Of course, Detective. This is my sister, Beth. Please sit down." Meg showed him into the living room. "Have a seat anywhere."

Detective Bohn sat in an easy chair. He turned his

hat this way and that. Meg wished that whatever he had to say, he'd spit it out. John would be home any minute, and he liked his dinner on the table at exactly five o'clock, which left her just forty minutes to get something together.

Beth finally broke the silence. "Would you like some coffee?"

"No thanks, ma'am." He cleared his throat, then began. "Mrs. Blackstone, your husband was involved in a bank robbery this afternoon, and has been arrested."

Meg sank into the nearest chair. "Involved? What do you mean 'involved'? Are you sure you have the right man?"

Detective Bohn explained that John and two other local men were suspected of being involved in several bank robberies over the past six years. Each one lived a life of respectability and had only been caught because the car they were driving had gone off the road in the midst of the police chase.

Meg leaned forward. "This can't be right. John works for the county. He has to go out of town sometimes."

She glanced at Beth. Truth be told, she didn't always believe he had to travel for work. Other men they knew never did. In fact, at one point, she'd wondered if he was having an affair.

"Your husband has never worked for the county. His overnight trips covered his robberies in other towns." He dug into his inside pocket. "I have a search warrant for the house and garage."

An affair she could believe. Some men were like that. Never could settle with one woman. But a criminal? No, she wouldn't believe that of him. "John wouldn't do those things." Even as she spoke, she heard the hollow ring to her words. She turned to her sister. "Beth, you know John. He couldn't do these things."

"The John I knew was a long time ago."

Beth's quiet response surprised her. No, angered her. "Thanks for nothing." She faced the detective. "Go ahead and search. You won't find anything, because there isn't anything to find."

The detective went to the door and motioned to several uniformed officers. Quietly and efficiently they went through the house. Meg and Beth sat awkwardly in the living room, not looking at each other, while the search progressed from room to room.

Beth cleared her throat after many long minutes of silence. "I'll leave if you want."

"Please don't." Panic rose in her at the thought of being alone. Of facing more questions. Of facing the neighbors. "I don't have anyone to turn to. Just wait and see. This is all a big mistake."

Meg looked around her once-familiar home as if

she were a stranger.

Oh God, I don't know where to turn. I need Your help. Please let this all be a bad dream. Please let me wake up now.

"I'll get us some coffee. Then we'll just sit and talk."

This wasn't a dream, It was real life.

Her life.

Meg remained in her seat, and tears began to flow. From the basement came muffled sounds of the continuing search.

Then, Detective Bohn came into the room, a folder of papers in his hand. "These bank statements show large deposits that coincide with unsolved robberies in the area. Since these accounts are all in your husband's name, it doesn't appear you were involved."

"Involved? You thought I might have been

involved?" The horror of her situation dawned on her as she stared out the kitchen window. The yard was dark, but not nearly as dark as her heart. "I never dreamt…"

Detective Bohn cleared his throat. "I'll be in touch tomorrow. Ma'am, since it appears that this house, the cars, all of this, is the result of criminal activity, you'll probably lose it. Bank robbery is a Federal offense, and the FBI will be here tomorrow. Once they begin following the paper trail, it's just a matter of time…" He looked at Meg. After she sat there for a moment with no reaction, he looked to Beth for help. "Will you stay with her? We don't like to see people alone at a time like this."

"Thank you, Detective. We'll see you tomorrow."

Beth took over the situation and shook hands with him, then showed him to the front door, where his fellow officers waited. She chatted with several she knew, one she'd even dated a few times.

Beth closed the door and went to the kitchen. A few minutes later, she returned to the living room with a cup of coffee for each of them and sat down next to Meg.

Meg sobbed quietly, and Beth reached around her to draw her close. They both sat in silence for some time, Meg dealing with the reality of the situation, Beth waiting patiently, coffee cooling on the table in front of them.

Finally, Meg raised her head, swiped at the tears running down her cheeks, and forced a smile. "C'mon. We have lots to talk about. Let's go into the kitchen."

The kitchen had always been a source of comfort for them. They'd spent hours together at this kitchen table, doing homework, planning which college to go to. Planning their weddings. It all seemed so long ago, and yet the pull to sit together again, at the same old scarred table, was strong.

They walked arm in arm, their laughter forced as

they tried to go through the kitchen doorway together. Meg poured out the cold coffee and filled the cups with hot java from the coffee maker then joined Beth at the table.

Sitting across from her sister, she met Beth's worried gaze. "What am I going to do, Bethy?" Her eyes filled again, as tears threatened to spill over once more. She pushed them back. "I don't have anyone else to turn to."

Beth sipped her coffee then set her cup down. "I've rehearsed this speech a hundred times. Now I don't remember where to start."

"How about at the beginning?"

"Do you remember what it was like, before I left?"

Meg nodded. "Some days it's all I can think about."

"No, I mean, do you really remember?"

Meg looked at her. "What do you mean?"

Her sister sighed. "You and me, always together.

Then the double wedding?" Meg nodded. "And I came to you before the wedding, and said we shouldn't go through with it?"

"I remember. I said 'I don't know about you, but I'm ready to be married.' And I was. John and I have had a wonderful life…"

"I found out what John and Tom were doing, and I knew I couldn't marry Tom, and I didn't want you to marry John."

"Tom is involved with this, too?" Meg couldn't believe it. John's little brother? The apple of his mother's eye. "I'm so glad his parents didn't live to see this."

Beth nodded. "I overhead him talking with John. Larry from the service station, too. They're all in it together. They were laughing about everyone being fooled. They needed to maintain a cover of respectability, and we were part of that cover."

"And you came to me, and I wouldn't listen."

"Yes. So I left. I should've told you."

"I should've trusted you enough to know more was going on than you were saying. Bethy, I'm not sure how this town is going to react when they find out the truth." Meg thought back to their younger days. She'd been so in love with John then. She sighed. So much had changed. "I don't know what I'm going to do. I've never had to work. John is—was—a good provider. But this won't destroy me, and it won't destroy us. That's the good thing about having a sister who is also your best friend. She always knows when she's needed the most."

Beth nodded. "I didn't know why, but like I said, God told me to come back. Now. Today. So I dropped everything and came."

"I'm so glad you're here." She stood and held out her hand. "Give me your cup, and I'll top that off. Then we need to think about what to have for dinner."

Beth checked her watch. "It won't be ready on time."

Meg shrugged. "Who cares? I'm not on a schedule. At least, not today." She turned to the counter, fighting back the tears she'd surely cry later. "Maybe we'll have popcorn."

"That's not much of a dinner."

Meg turned around to face her. "Hey, the prodigal sister has returned home, and I didn't have a fatted calf ready." She held up the coffee pot. "But I do have plenty of joe. So between you and me, we have all we need."

www.ingramcontent.com/pod-product-compliance
Lightning Source LLC
Chambersburg PA
CBHW071712020426
42333CB00017B/2235